Advance Pra... Don't Set Goals

Don't Set Goals (The Old Way) has caused a storm. Here are what business leaders are saying:

"Dear Wade:

Regarding your book **Don't Set Goals** *- the most important thing I think you can do to make it a best-seller, assuming you haven't already gone to press, is to make Chapter Seven, "Your Impossible Dreams," become Chaper One. It's so powerful because it tells your story and it shows that you can make it. As you know, more people read the first chapter than the last. I really love the part where you go through how you are going to build a billion dollar company."*

"To succeed extravagantly you have to study and be a mentee to a master mentor. Read this book, "Don't Set Goals" by one of the masters of our time, and you will get every good thing you want."

—In friendship, Mark Victor Hansen,
Co-Author of "Chicken Soup For The Soul"

"Finally, a focus on results rather than rhetoric, real achievement rather than the mere acknowledgment of attempt."

—Tracy Buhler, J.D.
President of U.S. Seminars

"Wade Cook has put it all together in a way that is clear. For decades the "rule" of success has been to set goals. Finally somebody is teaching us that the rule isn't "set goals," it's "succeed." I've given this to family and friends, and will give it to more. Thank you, Wade!"
—Scott Law, Gold Rhino Corporation

"During the last 18 years, my company, Education Leadership Dynamics, Inc. has helped 30,000 people take charge of their thoughts, attitudes and potential. I believe in actual change, actual progress, not in abstract and cerebral discussions. Thus I have never been a goal setter—but rather a goal-getter. As I read Don't Set Goals, I said to myself, "How is it that Mr. Cook could distill all my best thinking and experience into such a useful and readable book when he and I have never discussed this topic?" Clearly his life and experience have taught him the same lessons. I'm delighted he would write the book I wish I'd written. I'm even more delighted because he can reach hundreds of thousands of people with this vital message. Don't set goals—just get things done. Here's how. Here's why. Thanks, Wade."
—Joel D. Black, VP, CEO and General Manager, Education Leadership Dynamics, Inc.

"I firmly believe what Wade teaches in Don't Set Goals is extremely valuable. He hits it on the head with his theory that goals stop progress and

stagnate one's initiative. *Direction is the key. Thank you, Wade, for a new twist on life."*
—P. Cook, President,
Grand Teton Enterprises, Inc.

"Finally, a book that gets it right! I wish I could have read it 20 years ago!"
—Lance Strauss, CEO, Bedrock Corporation

"Once again, Wade Cook has challenged his readers to adopt a different mindset. I began reading his latest book, Don't Set Goals, with a bit of hesitation. I've always been a big believer in setting goals but I've now learned a way to immediately achieve these goals. It's not about goal setting, it's about goal getting."
—J.J. Childers, President and CEO,
Edge Funding Corporation

"Don't Set Goals was the first motivational book (and I've read hundreds) that I've read that truly made sense. The ideas set forth were practical, time tested and easily applied to dealing with the stresses of today's world."
—Kurt Bolinder, CEO, Master's Touch Inc.

Wade has absolutely hit a home run with this book! He incorporates ancient scripture to today's life—the truth is revealed."
—Pat James, President & CEO, Pabsba Corp.

Don't Set Goals
(The Old Way)

Wade B. Cook

Lighthouse Publishing Group, Inc.
Seattle, Washington

Printed in the United States of America

ISBN 0-910019-50-9 (pbk.)
Library of Congress Cataloging-in-Publication Data
Cook, Wade
Don't set goals : the old way / Wade B. Cook
p. cm. 1. Success--Religious aspects--Christianity.
2. Goal (Psychology) I. Title.
BV4598.3.C66 1997 158.1--dc21

"This publication is designed to provide accurate and
authoritative information in regard to the subject matter
covered. It is sold with the understanding that the publisher
is not engaged in rendering legal, accounting, or other
professional service, and is not intended to take the place of
such services or advice. If legal advice or other expert
assistance is required, the services of a competent
professional person should be sought."
— From a declaration of principles jointly adopted by a
committee of the American Bar Association and the
committee of the Publisher's Association.

Published by
Lighthouse Publishing Group, Inc.
14675 Interurban Avenue South
Seattle, Washington 98168-4664
(206) 901-3000
(206) 901-3170, fax
1-800-872-7411
www.wadecook.com
www.lighthousebooks.com

10 9 8 7 6 5 4 3 2

To all the people
who have gotten
in my way
and gotten out of my way.

They have helped me get
where I am.

To Ed Okazaki, in memory
To Dudley Rushton, Senior
To Earl Ewing
To Ralph Matteson, in memory

Acknowledgments

Fantastic!! We met our goal! This book is the product of quick, hard work, a product of what a college student would term an "all-nighter." I would like to acknowledge and give a heartfelt thanks to those on my staff whose dedication it is to help others get their goals. Lisa Michaels, my assistant, plays a double role and leads the team in my research/trading department and Wealth Information Network (WIN). Cheryle Hamilton, my executive officer at Lighthouse Publishing, is a terrific encourager and motivator. Jerry Miller, a faithful and loyal employee at Lighthouse Publishing Group, Inc., and the publications and graphics department who carefully proof and create the books I write, Mark Engelbrecht, Angela Wilson, Connie Suehiro, Brent Magarrell, Alison Curtis, Judy Burkhalter, and Chris Dalton have worked their hides off to get this book out. And to my wife, Laura, who encourages me supremely to BE my best and GET my goals, you're "maahvelous," darlin'!

Other books by Wade B. Cook:

Wall Street Money Machine
Stock Market Miracles
Bear Market Baloney

How To Pick Up Foreclosures
Real Estate Money Machine
Real Estate for Real People
101 Ways To Buy Real Estate Without Cash

Blueprints for Success
Business Buy The Bible
Brilliant Deductions
Wealth 101

555 Clean Jokes

Contents

Preface

It's a lot of fun to watch the eyes of seminar attendees as I say that one of the secrets to success is to not set goals. Many squirm uneasily until I replace the old worn-out "New Year's Resolution" concept with an infinitely better way to achieve success and happiness.

With all the books on motivational topics, all the success lectures in America and my goodness, all the day planners, you'd think that a vast majority of Americans would be successful. Alas, it is simply not true. Financially, 90% of all retirees have to substantially cut down on their standard of living. Crime is rampant. A smaller percentage of people attend church.

All those bad results amidst dozens of bestsellers. Something is wrong.

This is a fix-book, a how-to book. Specific problems will be isolated and discussed and specific solutions and methods for solving these problems will be put forth.

This author has been poor, then rich, then poor again, and now richer than he ever thought possible. Only a handful of basketball stars make as much money.

If you want to throw away the old stale ideas of success, you're invited to do so. If you want wild, yet simple, innovative, but functional ways to "be" successful, then this book is for you.

Rush Limbaugh was being praised one day by a caller who appreciated his sticking with it. He complimented Rush on making mistakes and moving on. Rush mentioned that another caller had asked him how to be successful in TV or radio— should he get with ABC, CBS, or NBC. I'm paraphrasing, but he said that one needed to define what success would be and approach it in that manner.

He told the story of his own career. If you want to respect yourself, like what you do, and be happy with that, then you would set about the process one way. He determined that he would get the largest listening audience by not catering to every desire or exploitation they or the mainstream media had for him.

If, however, you were looking for a career and defined it by how the honchos (media power brokers) in the New York, Washington D.C. axis felt about you, then you would play that game.

In this book you'll read my comments on success priorities; the first being to learn the formulas, or methods, or price to pay to make it. Follow these and you will be happier as you accomplish so much more.

You'll not get trapped in the never ending cycle of despair so prevalent today. Hope comes alive when you set about achieving wonderful things.

Here is an interesting thought: I went to different Bible dictionaries and concordances, even topical or word search guides. The word "goal" is not there. If the Bible doesn't use goals, why should I? Under direction, objectives, and motivations I found many great scriptures (See Chapter Nine), and they tell us how to act—how to succeed, God's way.

Time is short. Don't even wait to finish this book to put to work the principles found herein. I give them to you in the hope that finally you have and will use these tools to BE aware, BE happy and BE great!

Note: All references to Bible scriptures are from the King James Version.

"I've been married to this man for 15 years. Nothing about him is ordinary. He has never set a goal for himself. He simply sets out to do and to be what it takes to <u>achieve</u>. By doing so, he usually accomplishes far more than even he envisioned. This is the key to success in all areas of life."

—Laura M. Cook

1:
Don't Set Goals

"What we do upon some great occasion will probably depend on what we already are; and what we are will be the result of previous years of self-discipline."
—H.P. Liddon

Whenever I bring up this goal-getting approach I am criticized. Please don't get turned off by the title. Give me a chance to make a case for my idea. Dumping goal setting and coming up with a new M.O. (Modus Operandi, or Method of Operation) has served me well. It has made me millions. I know it will help you relieve stress, be happier, and currently and ultimately make you more successful.

I am really big into priorities. Priorities make or break you. They control your time and indeed, your whole direction. I will explain my love for priorities in a few pages. I'll add insights about targets and direction, but first let me blast away at typical feel-good goal setting strategies.

Simply put, I have a lot of problems with goals. First, they limit people; second, they set people up for failure; and third, they discourage many. I'll add another minor problem: sometimes goals take people in the wrong direction from where they want or need to be.

Don't quit trying to get to the Olympics, and don't drop out of college because of this. Goals can be okay for some people, but I contend that those who successfully achieve goals were driven in the first place. They were just that type of person.

Let me explain. Instead of setting goals, just be that kind of person. "To be" is an awesome

---

"It is not what he has, or even what he does which expresses the worth of a man, but what he is."
—Henri Frederic Amiel

---

concept. It is also difficult to appreciate so let's think it through. Instead of saying, "I want to be the high school quarterback," be that kind of person. Do what it takes to be the quarterback. Surround yourself with quality people that can help, people with experience, with insights, and with a determination to match yours.

Be, do—that's what it takes. Figure out the price you will have to pay in terms of practice, the elimination of free time, the new diet, the difficult regimen, the aches and pain—and the hurt if you're turned down. Ponder those things. Then start to work on and keep working on your resolve. It is your resolution that will see you through.

This word resolution has an interesting social aspect. I bring it up here because of its widespread

---

"Our grand business is not to see what lies dimly at a distance, but to do what lies clearly at hand."
—Thomas Carlyle

---

use and abuse. New Year's Resolutions. Every year they come up.

Tell me how many New Year's Resolutions you've made and broken, and that's how many reasons I'll give you why the traditional setting of goals is a waste. Goals (targets) are wonderful, but the way we go about setting them needs repairing.

I gave up these types of resolutions over 20 years ago. They don't work. I'm going to lose weight. I'm going to make a million bucks, and a thousand others.

You hardly hear things like this:

LOSE WEIGHT

1) I'm going to set my alarm at 5AM, get up, and walk or jog for 45 minutes.

2) I'm going to carefully select food at every meal with low fat content.

3) I'm going to get my resting heart rate down to 65 by doing 24 minutes of aerobics on Monday, Wednesday, Friday, and Saturday.

4) I'm going to plan my vacation and weekends around strenuous, muscle-stretching activities.

5) I'm going to do what thin (athletic or whatever) people do.

6) Nothing (activity) is more important than my health—nothing will get in the way—no excuses.

7) I'll work on my resolve—strengthen it every day to see this project through.

Talk is cheap. It is resolve and persistence which wins.

Sometimes just the mention of a new goal to family or friends gets all the accolades as if you finished the project. Pats on the back are the reward some people want—and it stops there.

To paraphrase a current sentiment: "Show Me the Fat Loss."

"Good thoughts, though God accept them, yet toward men are little better than good dreams except they be put in action."

—Francis Bacon

This is fun, so let's look at the would be millionaire. Remember when we were young and we wanted everything? I like that big house. I like that car. I like that girl. It's easy to talk the talk, a lot more difficult to walk the walk.

Lets get specific about making money.

I'LL MAKE MILLIONS

1) I'll read one or two financial newspapers every day. I'll read and study one book or three magazines in a week.

2) I'll seek out eight successful millionaires and learn everything I can. Financially, I'll avoid people who, "ain't making no money." Specifically, I'll seek people who can help in positive ways.

3) I'll learn specific formulas and use them in: a) my business, b) real estate, and c) the stock market. I'll develop habits which bring good results. I'll become a perpetual student.

4) I'll attend at least one seminar a month to get away, to learn new things, to meet new people, and to stay current.

5) I'll help my employees develop their skills by: a)_____, b)_____, c)_____ (you fill in the blanks).

6) I'll take care of my body and mind, as health and wealth are intertwined.

I could go on for several more pages, but I hope you get the point. Just BE. NIKE® says, "Just Do It." I like that slogan. I'll add "Just Be It."

Let me turn to the Bible for better clarification. I don't see a lot of goal setting going on. Matthew 5:48 says: "Be ye therefore perfect, as your Father which is in Heaven is perfect." This discussion can take two roads. We could concentrate on the word "Be," and we can discuss the word "perfect."

In the Hebrew language, there is no future time conjugation of the verb "to be." It is present tense. "I am that I am." The very essence of life—or God Himself. Being is where it's at. It doesn't say, "Set a goal to be," or, "try to be." It says, "be."

Later the question is asked, "What manner of person ought ye to be?" Not, "what should you set a goal to be," or, "try to be," or read some motivational book to get warm fuzzies for whatever you think is good. The answer: "even as I am."

Now, I'll deviate a little because I think a discussion of the word "perfect" is worthy at this point. The word "perfect" as used here is probably not the best usage or translation of the original Aramaic. Perfect as made in remarks about character is usually derogatory, or at least sarcastic, "Oh, you're so perfect, you do it." Even the word "perfectionist" has a slight negative connotation.

> *"We can do more good by being good, than in any other way."*
> *—Rowland Hill*

A different and perhaps more accurate translation would be "whole" or "complete." This is important to our discussion of goals in that when people realize that they cannot be perfect, they give up without much effort. "It's too difficult." "I can't do it." "Nobody's perfect." The battle is over before it begins. This was one of my reasons for not liking goals for a goal's sake.

I mentioned this in my book **Business Buy the Bible**. The root word of the words whole, heal, and holy is the same. Keep this in context for this discussion. The Bible from beginning to end is about healing, about repairing the rift between man and God. He did not cause it and wants us to change and become more like Him. Thousands of scriptures are given to help us learn His ways.

Those of us who are of Christ believe He came to heal this wound. In short, to make us whole. He prayed for unity, or for us to be one. I believe He went about healing the sick, the lame, the physically infirm to show that He can heal us spiritually.

"I have never heard anything about the resolutions of the apostles, but a great deal about their acts."
—H. Mann

Remember, the root word of heal is holy. If we can be healed through our repentance and submission of our will to His, and through His great gift of grace to us, then we can partake of His holiness. We become whole. I hope thinking of it this way helps. Now, everyday, we can do things which help this process or hinder it. That is why I'm so big on the precepts as taught in the Bible. The Holy Bible becomes the Healing Bible.

It's not so hard to "be" this type of person when we are given so much help. I would be remiss if I didn't mention the "Be-attitudes." What a beautiful collection of character traits we can work on, develop, and make better. There is a "whole," long list of things we can "be."

DO WHAT IT TAKES

When I was young I had an awesome youth church leader named Ed. We were very active. We had dozens of projects going on. Ed would give assignments and work with us to complete them. He would ask a boy to do something. The boy would say, "I'll try," or "I'll do my best."

Ed would lovingly jump all over them. "What do you mean you'll try? I don't want you to try, I

"Civilization varies with the family, and the family with civilization.—Its highest and most complete realization is found where enlightened Christianity prevails; where woman is exalted to her true and lofty place as equal with the man; where husband and wife are one in honor, influence, and affection, and where children are a common bond of care and love.—This is the idea of a perfect family."
—William Aikman

---

want you to do it. I need you to complete the task. What is your best, and what if that is not good enough? I might need you to be better than your best, to dig down and become better. I need you to complete the task."

I got my share of lectures and I just smiled and chuckled as the new guys got it. You see, within a week, I realized he was right. He never asked the impossible, though it definitely seemed that way at first. I grew up a lot under his tutelage. He was

> *"There is only one real failure in life that is possible, and that is, not to be true to the best one knows."*
>
> —Frederick William Farrar

great because he got us to do great things. To me he was a great man, because he did great things. "By their fruits ye shall know them." Ed brought forth good fruits. The seeds he planted are bringing forth even more good fruits. They will outlive him. He "tilled the earth" and made the garden more beautiful.

> *"Activity is God's medicine; the highest genius is willingness and ability to do hard work. Any other conception of genius makes it a doubtful, if not dangerous possession."*
>
> —Robert S. MacArthur

This has led me to look at great people and see what they accomplish. Great people accomplish great things.

I do not put myself in this category. But because of the success of my books and seminars and because of the awesome results so many are achieving, I hear, "You're great" quite often. It embarrasses me, and I don't know how to respond. To me, there is only one great man who walked this earth.

Maybe for lack of a better word, "great" is currently used. It has really caught me off guard. It's kind, but it has also given me pause for contemplation. What did I do or what can I do to be good for those people? It's simple. As a financial educator, I need to learn, explore, and teach the best methods I can to help people be better, to live better lives, to be better parents, to be a great spouse, boss, or friend. My job is not to see how much I can put into people, but to see how much I can get out of them.

What does this have to do with the word to "be?" I can't say I want to be the best financial teacher in America and not study the best, try the best, do the best. Every day I have to do great things. This is the career I've chosen. I love it. People count on me to be on the cutting edge. I work hard to anticipate people's needs, their problems, and their direction.

Being great means many things. I don't care what job you do, what hobbies you have, what in-

---

"The superior man is he who develops in harmonious proportions, his moral, intellectual, and physical nature. This should be the end at which men of all classes should aim, and it is this only which constitutes real greatness."

—Douglas Jerrold

---

vestments you make. It doesn't matter. What does matter is how you go about it. Mediocre effort gets mediocre results. Great effort produces great results. If you are a seventh grade math teacher, what are you doing now to be the best tomorrow?

Great ball players are always moving without the ball. What are you doing in preparation to be the best cheerleader in school? If you're on the chess club, what are you doing to make it exceptional? Or are you willing to settle for the status quo, for mediocrity—just to get by—the same old same old. There's no fun in a C average. Achieving is where the fun is.

To think of how I can be great, I have to think of my blessings. Then with each one, I, and I alone (with the help of prayer), decide if I want an A+ or a D-.

The first blessing is my knowledge of God and His will toward me. He knows me better than I know myself. He knows what road I should take. He knows what I need. I need to return this love. I need to care and share and give service. He has asked me "to love one another," and a host of other things. I owe it to Him to "walk uprightly," think on Him, repent quickly and completely, and endure well.

"The greatest and the most amiable privilege which the rich enjoy over the poor is that which they exercise the least,—the privilege of making others happy."

—Caleb C. Colton

You and I can be great as we magnify the Lord in our lives.

The next blessing is my wife and children. I am woefully inadequate, but with Heaven's help I'll keep improving. I want to be a great husband. I want meaning and passion and kindness to be in my marriage. I want my wife to feel special, like a queen. There are dozens of opportunities every day to do great (usually simple) things. Being great in this relationship produces wonderful, lasting results. No marriage should be devoid of trust.

The greatest thing a man and woman can give each other is complete loyalty and trust. I've seen too many otherwise happy marriages decimated by selfish acts. Even an appearance of impropriety (like simple flirting) is out of line.

Define greatness yourself. Remember when you first married? The love, the passion, the wonderful plans—the being together. Don't let it die.

Remember the words whole, heal, and holy, when enjoined to "cleave unto his wife" and to "one with another." Think of those words.

My kids need all the care, nurturing, and love they can get. I want to be a positive influence in their lives. I hope and pray they grow to love God in their youth. I hope the things I teach them, show them, and explain to them will stick with them.

I know they love me and think I'm a great dad, at least the little notes and cards say so, but this is one area where we can never do enough. Everyday I try to improve—to be the great dad they think I am.

My next blessing is my career and my business. My first responsibility is to my employees. We, as a company, have done and continue to do great and wonderful things. It's because of the great people there. I work hard at building a bigger pie. I want them to feel special. We help tens of thousands of people. How can I be good to our customers if I'm not good to the people I work with? As their lives improve, as they gain confidence, as they learn new things and expand their own horizons, then they are able to help others. I'm only one man. I can only be in one city at a time. Now I have dozens of instructors and other in-house staff which affect and influence many other lives.

All I have asked of my employees is to treat our company and our customers as they would want to be treated. In return, I want to treat them how I would like to be treated if our roles were reversed.

I want to be a true friend to my friends. I don't need to go to a seminar to learn this. Just concentrate on the word "be," and setting goals pales into insignificance.

SUMMARY

Many people use the words "set goals" as a convenience. Saying the words temporarily serves them. Even in my church, there is a lot of goal setting talk. Every time I hear it, I change it to

> *"The highest obedience in the spiritual life is to be able always, and in all things, to say, "Not my will, but thine be done."*
>
> —Tyron Edwards

goal getter. If you're going to set goals—then go get it. Do it. Be the kind of person that accomplishes what you set out to do. Ultimately, the process itself is important. In trying to be the quarterback, or be in a horse show, or have your own business, the improvement process is worthy of the effort. You'll learn more about yourself to be used in life's other conquests. To "be" is the key.

I dislike using the Army slogan as I was in the Air Force, but it does come down to this, "Be all you can be."

"If we work marble, it will perish; if we work upon brass, time will efface it; if we rear temples, they will crumble into dust; but if we work upon immortal minds and instill into them just principles, we are then engraving that upon tables which no time will efface, but will brighten and brighten to all eternity."

—Daniel Webster

2:
Goal Getter

"The large overriding question is this, 'Are you willing to pay the price?'"
—Wade Cook

My daughter, Leslie, loves horses. She would rather be with her horse than eat. My wife and other daughters, Carrie and Rachel, also love horses. They are very talented. We go to a lot of horse shows. They ride (English style) and show at Halter, and Leslie even jumps and goes on fox hunts.

We bought a 40 acre horse farm in the foothills of the Cascades, outside Seattle. We have room to run, jump, and practice.

Leslie wanted to go to the Youth National Arabian Horse Show in Oklahoma City. There, that's the target. Thousands of kids want to go, a few hundred actually do. If you want to call this a goal, then fine, but let's explore how it happens. By the way, at the time I wrote this, Leslie and the horse qualified to go. We're packing our bags.

The large overriding question is this, "Are you willing to pay the price?"

I even threw her a few curve balls. I'll go through the process. She rode in other shows. She's very talented and has a professional manner for one so young. She has style and grace. Her love of horses and focused attention allow her to be successful at this business—I dare not call it a hobby.

There were several things to discuss, but remember, the price to pay is the most important.

Question: What do you have to do to get ready?

Answer: Practice, train the horse, enter it in a qualifying regional show, and place first or second.

Question: How do you get first or second?

Answer: Buy a quality horse and practice many hours. Practice perfect moves.

Question: When do you have to do this?

Answer: In a timely manner to qualify for the big show. Also, each show (regional) has entry deadlines.

Question: What price is necessary?

Answer:

1) Any of several hours or days to train, groom, and study.

2) Miss out on activities with friends.

3) Have sore muscles, et cetera.

4) Be gone from home.

5) Entry fees and training money (Mom and Dad pay this).

"Learning, if rightly applied, makes a young man thinking, attentive, industrious, confident, and wary; and an old man cheerful and useful. It is an ornament in prosperity, a refuge in adversity, an entertainment at all times; it cheers in solitude, and gives moderation and wisdom in all circumstances."

—Ray Palmer

Then I throw in a negative. You know Oklahoma is mighty hot in July. "I don't care Dad, I want to go."

Now that we have discussed these things, we're ready to get on with it. To be a champion you must do what champions do.

Let me mention another workhorse. I'm always interested in the greatest. I study it. Today, Michael Jordan is the best basketball player in the world. Yes, he has innate talent. Yes, he's tall, but I'm impressed with how hard he works. I've read how he is often the first at practice and the last to leave. While others are wasting time, he's doing basic moves.

I'm impressed when I see multi-million dollar players doing lay ups and basic drills. They're great because they work at it. Michael Jordan is the best because *being* that is important to him. He excels because he does what it takes. He's a consummate individual and team player.

There are many other lessons we can learn from Michael Jordan and others, but the point of discussion is this, "Is he willing to pay the price?"

IN-HOUSE SALES

I get to work with an in-house sales staff. What wonderful people. Often they see others making big checks and want it. We teach basics, lay ups, chest passes, et cetera, and the ones who do them every day, make calls, send out letters, and answer the phone more often are the successful ones. Many are not willing to pay the price!

Michael Jordan may get two or three fantastic passes through thin air, flip the ball, turn around, change hands, slam dunks, but how many of his total points are simple (maybe to him, but impossible to me) jump shots or lay ups?

If a new person tells me they're going to make $10,000 a month (I have made way over this) I just smile and ask what they will do the next hour. What habits (boring though they may be) will they develop to generate that eventual income?

If they do have a successful pay period, they sometimes let up. A paycheck the next time around sharply lower than the previous one sends

---

"The real difference between men is energy. A strong will, a settled purpose, an invincible determination, can accomplish almost anything; and in this lies the distinction between great men and little men."

—Thomas Fuller

---

them back into their "lay up" reality. Lay ups, lay ups, I drill it in at every training session.

Wild goals cause failure. One time a young man came to my real estate seminar. He had a few thousand dollars to get going. That was more than I had to get started. He was excited at the end of the event. He bought all my books and courses and said, "I'm going to do 75 properties this year." He lived in Medford, Oregon. I said, "Just do one, do it right, then do a second one." He said he'd do more, there were so many deals in his town.

About six months later I was in Portland. He came up and reminded me who he was. I asked

---

"Anecdotes and maxims are rich treasures to the man of the world, for he knows how to introduce the forms at fit places in conversations and to recollect the latter on proper occasions."

—Johann Wolfgang von Goethe

---

about the 75 houses, and he told me he had done none. He stayed, and after the seminar I took him aside.

The conversation boiled down to this. I told him to go home (this was Saturday) and find one home and make an offer by next Thursday, then call me. He did. He sold one (that's my **Real Estate Money Machine** method) for about $6,000. This time I gave him marching instructions for one more. Within the next eight months or so he bought and sold 13 houses. It's not 75, but he made over $100,000. One deal at a time.

I don't want to hear about your goals. I want to see dedicated action. Don't tell me you want to develop a great personal relationship with God. Go get in your closet (quiet place) and pray. Stay there, return there often, and build that relationship one day at a time.

Don't tell me you're going to diet. Do what it takes. Losing weight and having a healthy body comes down to three things:

Proper attitude.

Proper nutrition.

Proper exercise.

All the diet books in the world boil down to these three. Learn them, get your resolve in gear, and do it.

Allow me to mention one by-product. Proper exercise, especially if it is walking, is wonderful for your success. Virtually every great thinker in the history of mankind walked a lot. Something to do with the movement of the spinal column and sacroiliac and other stuff. This is not an exercise book, but I thought I'd throw that in. Walk, and then walk some more.

"Every great man exhibits the talent of organization or construction, whether it be in a poem, a philosophical system, a policy, or a strategy.— And without method there is no organization nor construction."

—Edward George Bulwer-Lytton

Don't tell me you want to be a good manager if you're not willing to pay the price. It won't "just happen."

Don't <u>tell</u> me you're going to <u>set</u> a goal. <u>Show</u> me how you're going to <u>get</u> the goal.

3:
The Words I've Read

" ...she said, 'Your mind is like an attic. You can fill it with good junk or bad junk.'"

—Mrs. Halperin

The books I've read are like the food I've eaten. I don't remember them all, but they have made me what I am.

I'll never forget the day I got caught. A bunch of us in high school were always doing strange things. One day I hid a *Mad Magazine* inside a news magazine we were supposed to be reading in English class. Mrs. Halperin smashed it down in my lap.

I kinda liked her. She was old, I mean way old. She must have been teaching for a few hundred years. I was the teacher's pet. She liked me a lot more than I liked her. Maybe she saw something in me. Looking back I can see that, but that day became one of those memorable days—days which have an impact on the rest of your life.

She had two desks in the room, one in the front and one in the back. You see, it took so much energy for her to move from the back of the class-room to the front, that the move, once completed, required several minutes of recuperation. Did I say she was old?

This day she invited me to the back of the room. Most of the desks which were in use that period were towards the front. I thought I was really in for it. Getting old can bring on a certain harshness, maybe cynicism would be a better word.

Again, I thought it was off to the principal's office, or detention, or an extra assignment. Mrs. Halperin's punishments were swift and sure.

"The human mind cannot create any-thing. It produces nothing until after having been fertilized by experience and meditation; its acquisitions are the germs of its productions."
—Georges Louis Buffon

I sat in the chair beside her desk. My palms were as sweaty as Houston, Texas. The other kids really wanted to look back but didn't dare. Did I say she was mean? That's what I thought then. I was waiting for a good chewing out.

But do you know what followed? Compassion—maybe even caring would be a better word.

"Wade, I expect more of you. You're a leader. The kids look up to you." Then she lowered her head and in one moving gesture moved her chair closer to mine. Close enough so she could jab her index finger at the corner of my forehead. "Your mind is like an attic. You can fill it with good junk or bad junk." She talked on for a few minutes but I kept thinking about those words.

She took Alfred E. Neuman and threw him in the garbage can. "Don't put this garbage in your brain," were her last words that day.

The reason I paused and latched onto her words is because I had spent many hours in her class collecting sayings. You know, pithy little maxims that in a few words convey a major message

> *"Precepts or maxims are of great weight; and a few useful ones at hand do more toward a happy life than whole volumes that we know not where to find."*
> —Lucius Annaeus Seneca

or thought. I loved them. I even had a place in my notebook where I would write them down.

My English teacher one year earlier got me started. Every day he had a new one on the blackboard up in the corner of the room. These meant a lot to me. So much so that I memorized many of them. For example, the Tacoma Washington Lincoln High School Class of 1917 had as their slogan, "If there's a way, take it; if not, make it."

This statement has meant so much to me. Every time I'm down, I think of it. It has meant so much to me that I put it at the end of the first chapter of **Real Estate Money Machine**, my first book. I wasn't, and still don't consider myself to be, an author. I had no idea how to write or what to write in that first book. That was almost two decades ago and it's still selling in the bookstores.

I accomplished building my first fortune, starting with a borrowed $500, against all odds, with no discernible path to walk down. I had to make my own way. Many more of these sayings, including proverbs, had major and minor impacts in my life. They helped me forge my character. I want to share one more with you and then tell you a realization I recently had the fortune of discovering—this discovery has been 30 years in the making. I'm amazed at God's patience with me.

> *"I would fain coin wisdom,—mould it, I mean, into maxims, proverbs, sentences, that can easily be retained and transmitted."*
>
> —Joseph Joubert

SERENDIPITY

I have been blessed by a serendipitous life, too many coincidences to write off as luck or fate.

Serendipity is defined as a happy or joyous discovery found on the way to something else. For example, a new friend is found when you join the volunteer fire department, or a solution to a computer problem comes to you when you're fixing your boat. The list goes on. All of us have had them. Sometimes they happen every day. One of my living methods is to live a serendipity guided life. I even pray for such experiences.

We all seem to grow rapidly at first, then slowly. We embrace change reluctantly, so we miss many opportunities to act and to be acted upon. Serendipitous experiences abound and await our simple recognition.

Another powerful expression, or maxim, came into my life which not only changed my life, but countless tens of thousands of others. This had to do with real estate. Again, from a financial point of view, real estate was my first love.

"The value of a maxim depends on four things: its intrinsic excellence or the comparative correctness of the principle it embodies; the subject to which it relates; the extent of its application; and the comparative ease with which it may be applied in practice."

—Charles Hodge

The game was to buy rentals. Every book, every seminar, everything in real estate was some variation of the rental game. I saw my way out of poverty. The books said I could play this rental game with no money (I qualified), no credit (I was a broke cab driver), and no experience (to the "T").

I became a student of the process. Within one year I owned nine rental houses. I beat that cab to death to get money for down payments, closing costs, and even paint and carpet. I was soon worth $120,000. That was big time money for me. It was 1977, a working class town, and I was just beginning. I saw that I could be a millionaire within three to five years.

I had a hidden agenda which is not important to this story, so I'll mention it briefly here and pick it up later. I invested in real estate so I could generate enough income to finish college so I could become a college professor. Ever since I was 16 I knew I wanted to teach—hopefully teach money and business.

I did not do real estate to do more real estate. I mentioned I saw myself becoming a millionaire. That is partially true. I thought of it once in awhile. Who doesn't? I wanted it all, but from a youthful point of view.

It was not my passion. I wanted to teach. I became a millionaire, but I lost it all very quickly. That is another story that I'll tell you the details of later. Just remember that my driving force was not the accumulation and preservation of assets—not the first time around.

Back to the real estate story. I was, by most yardsticks, successful. My net worth was growing but the cash flow dried up. If you've had rentals, you'll relate. I had assets. I had equity, but one bad month (even one vacancy) can wipe out your profits. Here I was worth $120,000, and a $65 electric bill came due and I had no way to pay it.

The rental game wasn't all that it was cracked up to be. I met very few people who were consistently successful over a long period of time. Those who were had a lot of cash on hand in rental property with no or small loans. Don't get me wrong, it can be done, but I was impatient.

Again, I wasn't doing the rentals for wealth, but for income. I wanted to create enough monthly net cash flow to support my young family as I went back to college. I almost achieved it several times, only to have it slip away.

That is where *Forbes Magazine* came in. I loved that magazine—even at the age of 20. I still do. Malcolm Forbes, the founder, the father of Steven Forbes, said (and I'm paraphrasing), "No success is ever accomplished by a reasonable man." Wow, that hit me like a ton of bricks. Let me say it again, "No success is ever accomplished by a reasonable . . . woman."

A lot of doubt had crept into my life about that time. I was embarking on a path that others thought foolish. I violated everything the books said to do. I was contrary to the "established" law of real estate investing. I literally had people call me names.

"There is nothing so elastic as the human mind. Like imprisoned steam, the more it is pressed the more it rises to resist the pressure. The more we are obliged to do, the more we are able to accomplish."
—*Tryon Edwards*

What I wanted to do didn't seem crazy to me. Here was my simple plan. I had bills to pay. I had equity in these houses. I would sell one, pay the bills, and hopefully use the leftover cash to buy more properties. It seemed simple. Everyone told me not to do it. "Buy real estate and wait," was another saying on my office (back bedroom) wall. It comes from the statement, "Don't wait to buy real estate, buy real estate and wait."

Hook, line, and sinker, I was into real estate <u>their</u> way. Now my books and methods have been so overwhelmingly successful that I refer to this "buy and hold" strategy as old fashioned. Oh, it has its place, but it was not working for me in a way that would let me accomplish what I needed it for.

I put a house up for sale. The buyer was getting a loan. He qualified. The house didn't. I ended up taking his down payment and carrying back the mortgage—owner financing, if you will. I had no idea I could do it or how to do it. It just happened by good people at the title/escrow company. I became his banker. I had my cash back, but mind you, not as much as if I would have gotten all cash from a totally financed deal.

Oh, how I needed that cash. Instead, I ended up with something better. A mortgage with monthly checks and a great lesson in life. Serendipity strikes again.

What I discovered was really cool. For example, you know that rule (law) on calculation that says you'll pay three times for a house: $200,000 will cost over $600,000 because of the 30 year cost of carrying a mortgage for so long (Oh, by the way, see the appendix in **Business Buy the Bible** on how to pay off this debt faster.)

Now that I'm the banker I'll get all that interest (unless the loan pays off early). Also, the payments coming in were higher than the rent payments. People will simply pay more to buy than to rent. My asset sheet looks good—a hard "to-the-penny" note receivable, not a nebulous value. Yes, I would lose the appreciation, but I got my cash back. I could eliminate some bills, then buy more.

I would also have a blend of properties. So here's what happened. It was the discovery of the greatest serendipity of all. This process could be designed and duplicated. Again, if one gets back all his cash, he can do it again.

Cash in, cash out (usually more) and you leave behind a note, secured against the property, churning out a $195 monthly check (or whatever). Do 20 to 30 of these and it's "retirement time."

In short, you could get good at the process. Work it. It has a clean beginning, middle, and end. Repetition and duplication are one major key to wealth.

What started out as a simple move to get cash to pay some bills turned into a publishing and seminar empire. Hundreds of thousands of people have read and used these cash flow strategies. My book, the ***Real Estate Money Machine***, is going on 20 years and its 15th printing. This truly was a happy and joyous discovery.

Malcolm Forbes's words rang true to me then, as they do now. They helped me stick out, break out, and go against the conventional wisdom of the time. Yes, they're just words, but words have meaningful results as we employ them in our activities.

"Be methodical if you would succeed in business, or in anything.—Have a work for every moment, and mind the moment's work.—Whatever your calling, master all its bearings and details, its principles, instruments, and applications.—Method is essential if you would get through your work easily and with economy of time."
—William Mathews

TO THE POINT
Our brains are like giant computers, but better in many ways. If you want good results, put good things in your brain.

Now that I'm an adult, I have reread many of those same ideas in new books. No kidding, a joke told in 1957 has found its way into current literature. But I've also noticed something else, something very interesting and important.

Many of the quotes, the stories, the ideas that I thought were original to those authors are found in the Bible. It seems to be the greatest success, motivational, personal development book of all time. The genesis of all this good is in the Scriptures (no pun intended).

Can you find me a better book? I don't think you can. It is interesting, it is fun, and it is definitely intriguing. It has love stories, good and bad guys, it has wars, peace, friendships, and betrayals. It is the Book of Life.

So my natural conclusion is this: if it's the best place to go, if so many authors quote from it, paraphrase it, if it's used in our Constitution, our country, our whole way of life (though there are some who want it destroyed or abandoned), then why not read it more, use it more.

Awhile ago I wrote **Business Buy the Bible**. I quoted directly. I don't want to hide those verses. I have been criticized and will be criticized more, but, my intent is firm: to get people to buy the Bible, then buy into and use its messages. I'm confident that anyone who does so will grow immensely. You see, we can then see past these motivational weirdos and seek a higher source which will bring about real change.

> "There can be no end without means; and God furnishes no means that exempt us from the task and duty of joining our own best endeavors. The original stock, or wild olive tree of our natural powers, was not given us to be burnt or blighted, but to be grafted on."
> —Samual Taylor Coleridge

4:
Direction

"In my company I'll give my back forty acres for a loyal, enthusiastic person."

—Wade Cook

I have a good friend named Nick. He flies for a major airline and also has a tropical flower farm in Hawaii. He is very astute and not only a thinker, but a doer, a rare mixture of qualities.

We met at one of my seminars, and though I don't become close friends with many of my attendees, I, actually we, as my wife joined in, have become friends with Nick and his wife, Judi.

I invited Nick to be on the Board of Directors of our parent company, which is publicly traded. He has served with dedication and exuberance. I have enjoyed his ideas, his feedback, his caring, and concern.

We have many discussions, usually about the Bible, but often on business. I mentioned in one of my seminars that direction was more important than speed, because Nick loves to fly and it shows.

I asked him about getting off course and the corrections necessary to correct problems. The scenario was a flight from Los Angeles to New York. A small error, left uncorrected, a wind change or other traffic could put the plane off course. If uncorrected for a long period of time the results would be dramatic.

Even a very small degree change, if prolonged, would leave the plane way off course. I know this would never happen, but imagine the New York bound plane ending up in Washington D.C. or Boston. They are hundreds of miles from New York. But from Los Angeles, a slight shift would take you over Riverside instead of San Bernardino.

The angle is the key. A large degree variance has an exponential effect later. I mean, the plane could end up in Miami. On the other hand, the problem at the beginning is simple to correct, with the right instruments and right people.

Think of the cost of correcting a major mistake. The fuel from Washington, D.C. back to New York is costly. Think of the angry passengers. Now, I know this won't happen, but the point, I hope, is made.

In life, as in business, we need to constantly make corrections. If the direction is good in the first place, if we still want the intended results, then all sorts of things will arise to help and hinder the process.

But give me a man or woman with a mission, and it's as if the very forces of nature will lie down to allow the accomplishment of the task.

"That discipline which corrects the eagerness of worldly passions, which fortifies the heart with virtuous principles, which enlightens the mind with useful knowledge, and furnishes to it matter of enjoyment from within itself, is of more consequence to real felicity than all the provisions which we can make of the goods of fortune."

—Hugh Blair

A person with a mission, a passion and enthusiasm, is a sight to behold. In my company I'll give my back forty acres for a loyal, enthusiastic person. You can measure the success of the direction you're going by how well your passion is sustained. If it wanes, then check your integrity level. Is what you say, do, and think, all the same? Keep this in alignment.

By saying direction is more important than speed, I do not mean to imply that speed is not important. One maxim I've used at my seminars and in other books is this,

"If you'll do for two years what most people <u>won't</u> do, you'll be able to do for the rest of your life what most people <u>can't</u> do."

In our fast paced society, our attention span has decreased. If you read my financial books you'll hear me talk about "two years" quite often. For example, I have a web site where I list almost all of my trades, plus our instructors trades and dozens of other information tips. Through our website, people can subscribe to **WIN** (Wealth Information Network) for this information. We sell the package by the year. Many of our students subscribe to WIN so they can look over the shoulder of a millionaire and his staff. It's a very popular service, but I tell them, "Okay, buy one year, maybe two, but if you haven't gotten rich in that time using my formulas, you'll probably never make it. Go do something else."

If you go about a task and you don't see results right away, you'll probably get discouraged and quit. That's why speed and results are important.

My daughter gets a lot of feedback, results, and ribbons on her way to Youth Nationals. I don't know how she or anyone can achieve great things without feeling a sense of accomplishment.

I'm reminded of a story learned long ago about the woman trying to swim the English Channel. The day she set out was very foggy. After a few miles she tired and quit. On a clear day, when she could see way out, she made it.

Goals, tasks, or targets have to be definable, achievable and then done with adequate speed in the proper direction.

"Know thyself," said the old philosophy.—"Improve thyself," saith the new.—Our great object in time is not to waste our passions and gifts on the things external that we must leave behind, but that we cultivate within us all that we can carry into the eternal progress beyond."

—Edward George Bulwer-Lytton

5:
Whatcha Gonna Do, Jack? Whatcha Gonna Do?

"It seems half the successful people I talk to stumbled into it or did it by accident."

—Wade Cook

I was having lunch recently with a fairly successful sales representative for a business television station. I only mention this because he associates with thousands of business people—people from major companies—and every kind of entrepreneur in between.

We were sharing ideas about my "**Don't Set Goals**" concept and he, almost like everyone else, was taken aback. He tried to argue and started talking about success and why people don't make it. I could hardly wait for him to pause so I could ask him what he did to be successful. I'll get to that in awhile.

He said that everyone knows how to make it, to be a success, they just don't do it. I couldn't buy into his supposition, but even if I did tie the

---

"Man was born to be rich, or grows rich by the use of his faculties, by the union of thought with nature. Property is an intellectual production. The game requires coolness, right reasoning, promptness, and patience in the players. Cultivated labor drives out brute labor."
—Ralph Waldo Emerson

---

two together (that they know how to do it, but don't), it would still prove my point, and prove it in a big way.

Using my best "kindly debate" tactics, I tried to get a word in. I respectfully disagreed. My experience in the real world, I said, tells me people don't know how to do it. "It" meaning: be successful, lose weight, get rich, or any other realistic goal. It seems half the successful people I talk to stumbled into it or did it by accident. Many wealthy people are so because they were in the right place at the right time. Their personal efforts or talents had not even an iota of importance to the process.

I pressed on. To me, very few successful people or companies had a game plan, and if they did in the beginning, they were not currently doing what they originally set out to do. Facts from other collected data bear this out. Many inventions, or discoveries, things we use and take for granted (penicillin, laser discoveries, global positioning systems) are the by-products of other technologies—and some stumbled on by complete accident. Lucky for us someone was astute enough to see the possibilities.

"One of the things I teach at our Wall Street Workshop is to bet on the jockey, not on the horse."
—Wade Cook

He was not swayed. He firmly believed when I finished that "not doing it" was sine qua non to failure. I can't disagree totally, because even if people know how to do it, or what to do to make it, most don't. Now, by writing the word "most" in the last sentence it may seem that many people or "most" people know how. I say very, very few people know how to be truly successful. And of the few that know how, only a handful are truly happy when it happens. But happiness is a discussion we'll deal with in other works.

Also, I want to clear up a misconception that may occur if the reader thinks that what I wrote a few paragraphs ago about companies and people changing or not doing what they set out to do, means that I don't like change, creativity, or innovation.

If a person needs a detailed plan about what we're trying to accomplish, how we're going to make, promote, and distribute widgets, a plan to be successful or to get started on the road, then great. If it doesn't work, adapt, change, modify, innovate, and push on. Success and development of personal traits is important to me. One of the things I teach at our Wall Street Workshop is to bet on the jockey, not on the horse. I like success even if it comes after several setbacks. Get started and make changes along the way. It's called "production towards perfection." As my good friend Robert Hondel says, "Let Serendipity take care of it."

BOOTSTRAPS—HIGH HIGH BONUSES

Back to my discussion with my friend. I told him that at my financial seminars we give specific formulas for making money. These formulas, methods, and techniques are well defined, easy to understand and easier to implement. They are time tested. I ask people who tell me that at the two day event they made back the tuition and were ahead $6,400, or $8,200, or $1,400, what specific formula they used. They can explain it in detail. They bought the stock at $14.25 (rule one for covered call writing: buy in the $5 to $25 range), they bought on margin (rule two: only half the money is needed); they waited for the stock to rise to $15 or $16 (rule three: buy stocks which are volatile and roll or trade between a certain range), and then sell the $17.50 call the next month out (another short trade technique) and capture the $1.50 ($1,500 cash if ten contracts were sold) thereby getting a 20 to 40% one month gain (40% or even 60%) if called out (sell the stock).

They are happy as can be. They learned the formulas and the rules well. They experienced success and most importantly, they can repeat the process. If, as I've said so many times, one key to success is duplication and repetition, then they are well on their way.

Conversely, once in awhile, I talk to someone who loses money on a trade. These stories are so few and far between that I really don't know how to handle them. I emphasize, we never promised 100% successful trades. We don't make recommendations.

Here's how it goes. "What strategy did you use?" "I was doing an option on a stock split." "OK, what was your plan?" "Just to make money." "Now specifically, which of the five times to do options on stock splits were you doing? Did you check the charts and the fundamentals? What was your exit point?" (I'm really big into "know your exit before you go in the entrance.") "Uh, uh, I don't know."

You see, that's not what we teach at the event. It's not what we do. If the person said this, "I bought the June 55C (call option) on XYZ for $2\frac{3}{8}$. I was planning on a $2 to $3 jump in the stock the day or two before, on the split or ex-dividend date. That would push the option to $3\frac{3}{8}$ and I'd get out at $1 profit ($500 or $1,000 or $10,000—depending on the quantity of contracts). This strategy

---

> *"The first law that ever God gave to man, was a law of obedience; it was a commandment pure and simple, wherein man had nothing to inquire after or to dispute, for as much as to obey is the proper office of a rational soul acknowledging a heavenly superior and benefactor.—From obedience and submission spring all other virtues, as all sin does from self-opinion and self-will."*
>
> *—Michael E. de Montaigne*

---

follows our model. If it doesn't perform as expected, learn from it and get on. You know I never get an answer like this. Losing comes from not following the rules, or a weird drop in the stock or market.

Now, some of you just estimated that at $2\frac{3}{8}$, $2,375 would be lost—either partially or in total if the play doesn't work. Maybe you can't afford to lose that much. Okay, so let me tell you about Beth Anne. She came to the WSWS (Wall Street Workshop) and lost $2,980. She was devastated. Her husband was not happy. I read her letter, a chronology of trades, four total trades made at the WSWS. The day after the class the market dropped 120 points. Her particular option did not have enough time to recover. She actually started with $3,700 and lost $2,980. That's sad.

I asked her, "Did not the instructor explain to you diversification? Did he not use the examples of $5,000—if you have $5,000 to get started only $500 or $1,000 should be in options" (and only then if this is risk money, or money you don't need)? "Did he not explain how risky options are?" (Yes, they are great money makers but they have a downside risk.)

"Success and happiness come from the proper application of knowledge."

—Wade Cook

She answered, "Yes, yes, yes," to all of these questions. She blew it. She did not follow the most fundamental rules. She jumped in, but should have a) diversified, b) only used risk capital, c) gained more experience by paper trading, or doing one trade at a time to gain experience.

Many years ago I bought a restaurant. The previous owner told me that if the recipe for chowder called for a tablespoon of salt, the hardest thing he did was to get an employee to put in an exact tablespoon of salt. Not a palmful, not a heaping spoonful, not a guesstimate, but an exact tablespoon full.

I agree, getting our students to follow exact directions is often as difficult.

Just having knowledge is not a guarantee of success. Many doctors know how harmful smoking is but smoke anyway. Success and happiness come from the proper application of knowledge. Some call this wisdom.

SUMMARY
Learn the formulas (rules) that you must follow to be successful.

Set a course.

"Aim at perfection in everything, though in most things it is unattainable; however, they who aim at it, and persevere, will come much nearer to it, than those whose laziness and despondency make them give it up as unattainable."

—Philip Dormer Stanhope Chesterfield

Define as many obstacles as possible and how you'll solve problems. In fact, you'll be way ahead in life if you figure out what kind of problems you like to solve, or work on, and then get into that business.

Get up your resolve. List clearly what you have to do, are willing to do, and decide who needs to do it.

Get on with it. Life is not complicated. Yes, you have to do it, but you have to know what to do and get good at learning the formulas (methods, techniques).

To do well at everything listed above you need to excel at setting priorities. The next chapter deals with this.

"What we truly and earnestly aspire to be, that in some sense we are.— The mere aspiration, by changing the frame and spirit of the mind, for the moment realizes itself."

—Mrs. Jameson

6:
Priorities

*"Here I was violating what I teach.
Don't tell me, just do it."*
—Wade Cook

When people ask me, "Well, if you don't like goals, what do you like?" I say, "PRIORITIES." And then I have to remind them I love goals. I think targets, goals, and direction are wonderful. The title to this book does not say, "Don't Goals," It definitely doesn't say "Don't Succeed." In fact, the mission of this book is to help you succeed and be happy beyond your wildest dreams.

It's the "setting" goals process that I think fouls things up. Too much lip service and talk is cheap. Let me give an example of the here and now. Today is Friday. I just flew to Los Angeles to do a taped TV show. I'm on the plane going home.

Monday, I flew to New York, Philly on Wednesday, home Thursday, and back home Friday night. I hardly ever travel anymore so it's been a busy, yet wonderful, week.

On the way home from Philly, I wrote three chapters, "Don't Set Goals," "Goal Getter," and "The Words I've Read." This book was never designed to be a 200 to 300 page book. As a matter of fact, it will be my first paperback book—out first in paperback, that is. There is a major reason for this. If I'm successful, I'll tell about it in another book, or in a subsequent edition of this book. It has to do with the NYT (New York Times).

"Great opportunities come to all, but many do not know they have met them.—The only preparation to take advantage of them, is simple fidelity to what each day brings."

—Albert Elijah Dunning

I've written (by hand) about 65 pages this week. That translates into about 50 to 60 pages in a book, depending on the size.

I was going to finish the book by Monday and give it to the production staff at Lighthouse Publishing. Yesterday, Thursday, in a brief production meeting, I let it slip that I had written about half of a new book. They thought it was my new Stock Market book, or my success book. Little did they know I started to write that book. It was my goal, but as I started writing, my passion was to write **"Don't Set Goals (The Old Way)."** I've thought of this book, lectured on these concepts, and employed them for twelve years.

They had never heard this title and they were shocked. Maybe pleasantly surprised would be better. I told them it would be completed by Monday. Here I was violating what I teach. Don't tell me, just do it.

Now I was in a dilemma. I decided to turn it into a test. Can I say I'll finish another four or five chapters in four days? Or would I be another person saying, "I'm going on a diet." Part of the difficulty is that one of my best friend's entire family is moving this weekend. They're staying at our house until the plane leaves. A few hours before that our national speaker trainer is coming to town with his wife for a week. I promised them and my kids we'd go to the lake Saturday afternoon for some boating. Also, I've got to look at a new building for a headquarters location of our Financial Education Centers, and on top of that I just bought a '59 Corvette convertible and I want to go cruising.

Whatcha gonna do Wade? Whatcha gonna do?

So here I am on the plane, dead tired, forcing my eyes to stay open to write two more chapters. Tomorrow, Saturday, I'll get up at five or six AM

"All I have seen teaches me to trust the Creator for all I have not seen."

—Ralph Waldo Emerson

---

and write two to three more chapters. That means I have to forgo my Friday night movie date with my wife. We'll go to two next Friday, but this book will be done by Monday.

Now, why am I telling you all this? All of us have a myriad of things that can take up our time. We excel at making excuses. At one of my real estate seminars a wise elderly woman, one who had made hundreds of thousands of dollars with my real estate strategy, said, "You can make money, or you can make excuses, but you can't make both." What a powerful concept.

What gets in your way? What are your road blocks—both real and imaginary? What stops you?

There is nothing I can say at this time other than to set your priorities. I dealt with setting priorities from a spiritual perspective in *Business Buy the Bible*. Now we'll deal with them for daily living.

"You will never 'find' time for anything. If you want time you must make it."

—Charles Buxton

H.L. Hunt, the famous billionaire, was asked on a talk show why he was so successful. He said there were four things:

1) Decide what you want.

2) Decide what you'll give up.

3) Set your priorities.

4) Be about it.

"The sons of the rich, the educated darlings of wealthy families, are nowhere.—All their gifts were only so many fatal temptations, and they themselves are forgotten, like bad copies of good pictures."

—John W. Forney

This is an awesome plan. Remember this was said by the guy who made all the money. Don't confuse him with his kids who lost it all, and filed bankruptcy. You see, he understood principles of wealth. They were real to him. He learned them from others, from experience—from walking the walk.

His kids obviously did not "get it," so they don't get to "keep it."

Let's review what he said. The first thing was to decide what you want. Heavens, everyone does that. "I want to be rich," "I want success," "I want to be President," "I want to be them," that's easy.

The next step is a tough one. What must you do? What are you willing to give up? What price has to be paid? And is it worth it? This is where most falter. If one does not have sufficient resolve, or sufficient tenacity then steps three and four will fall apart.

Boy, when he got to step number three, I'm sure glad he said, "Set your priorities" instead of "set your goals." This says succinctly what I practice and what I teach.

Here is a helpful way to stay on track with your priorities. Consistently ask yourself:

What else could I be doing with my time?

What else could I be doing with my money?

If you ask these questions and honestly answer them, then you'll realize that you and your time have (like real estate) a highest and best use. Trouble is, we spend so much time doing wasteful, nonsensical things. Time flies and we can't recapture it. It's like an airplane flying with empty seats, or a hotel with empty rooms, never again will there be a time when yesterday's empty seat or room can be sold.

What else? It's a powerful question. Ask it about ten times a day and then do your answer—be the answer. Do your highest and best use.

And then I absolutely love his part four: be about it.

"Be," a curious word, a word that needs to find added dimension in our pursuit of happiness.

Be true to yourself.

Be there, or be square.

"To be, or not to be."

One last helpful hint. If you combine these two strategies from this chapter and the chapter entitled "Whatcha Gonna Do"—whenever we talked about discovering your own "How to," or "What to," then one top priority should be to learn <u>what it takes</u> to get you to your target. A continuing priority should be the ongoing acquisition of information to help you improve and BE better.

"If you want to succeed in the world you must make your own opportunities as you go on. The man who waits for some seventh wave to toss him on dry land will find that the seventh wave is a long time a coming. You can commit no greater folly than to sit by the roadside until someone comes along and invites you to ride with him to wealth or influence."

—John B. Gough

7:
Impossible Dreams

"You can practice something wrong all day long and still have it wrong."

—Wade Cook

The past two decades of my life have been most interesting. I've done so much it seems like two lifetimes. In all of this I have become a student of people—of successes and failures. The magazines I read, the articles in newspapers, the books I read and have in my reference library, and the TV and radio I watch and listen to focus on people. Cause and effects.

I want to be sure that what I'm feeding into my own mind, and my soul, and consequently what I do and become and then teach to others, is the truth.

Gaining knowledge is worthy of the goal, but as the years pass, knowledge changes. Look what we know about the sea, space, even our own bodies, now as compared to 200 years ago. Medical practice by the best physicians around this country's revolutionary period would seem barbaric today. So yes, knowledge is important, but so much more valuable if we keep it in perspective—stand on its shoulders to see higher and farther. Truth, however, never changes. One's perception of truth, what we do with it, how it is acquired, and how knowledge is filtered is in a constant state of flux. This process needs scrutiny.

For example, we feed our brains lies all of the time. We learn, or think we learn, certain maxims, rules, or methods only to find out we don't really grasp them, or "get it" at all. Look at some of our accepted notions and how wrongly devastating they can be.

IT TAKES MONEY TO MAKE MONEY
Yes, this is true, but it's a half truth, a statement incomplete. Yes, it takes money, but not your money. Fortunes are built with other people's money. I wonder how many fortunes (business, careers, et cetera) are not even commenced upon because this statement was used to shut them down, to stifle a beginning.

PRACTICE MAKES PERFECT
Not really. You can practice something wrong all day long and still have it wrong. Perfect practice, or effective practice makes perfect.

> "It is not so difficult a task to plant
> new truths as to root out old errors,
> for there is this paradox in men: they
> run after that which is new, but are
> prejudiced in favor of that which is
> old.
> A truth that is merely acquired from
> others only clings to us as a limb added
> to the body, or as a false tooth, or a
> wax nose. A truth we have acquired
> by our own mental exertions, is like
> our natural limbs, which really belongs
> to us.—This is exactly the difference
> between an original thinker and the
> mere learned man."
> —Arthur Schopenhauer

You can see the point. Half truths, mis-truths throw us off as much as outright lies. They affect the brain in many irretrievable ways. Look at this next statement. It is probably one of the most widespread sayings around. It is used in many situations to basically say you can't have it all. God wants us to have it all. Said the wrong way (which everyone does) it is devastating. Said the right way, the original way, it makes sense and then, by the way, becomes part of a priority setting process.

Here is what we say:

"You can't have your cake and eat it too."

It's just pure hogwash. Why are we feeding our brains such a lie? Think about it. Can you have a cake and eat it? Sure you can. Then why say this?

The way it is supposed to go is:

"You can't eat your cake and have it too."

Now this makes sense. There are consequences. If you eat it, it's gone. You can't still have it. If you spend money, if you use up time, it's gone. If the sentence were changed to, "You can't have your cake if you eat it," then truth would be restored.

I'm doubtful if you can henceforth use this statement like you have in the past. It's so common. It's in two rock and roll songs I know of. A radio commentator used it yesterday. I wanted to call and correct him. Yes, he used it to prove a point, wrongly, that you can't do two things.

Why am I bringing all this up here? Because one such statement that I think throws people off track is the expression about goal setting.

It's as if the very act of setting goals becomes a substitute for achievement. Goal setting becomes an end in and of itself. The sweet smell of victory rarely occurs because people get caught up in a process which seldom works.

I stated earlier that I have three problems with goal setting the traditional "New Year's Resolution" way.

First, setting goals this way sets people up for failure. The very nature of the process means people haven't taken the time to dream, to ponder, to actualize the results. They don't know all the obstacles. They don't ascertain how they will deal with changes, with problems, and with new opportunities.

Very little thought goes into changing ourselves. Our methods are not given scrutiny. Improving and "being" better is worthwhile. Learning new and wonderful things along the way, like new friends, new processes, new solutions, is given little thought.

The end, whether justified or not, whether proper or not, overshadows everything.

Does the end justify the means, or the means justify the end? In most endeavors, the means justify (make possible) the end. Then dream of where you want to go. Ponder its implications and go for it—set out on the journey, but make the journey wonderful. Very few businesses or careers are freeways to success. There are many setbacks, many trials, many disappointments—those are not only part of the process; they make the outcome what it will be.

Goal setting, the old way, is insignificant to making it happen. Goal getting will make it happen.

You may have a setback, but you don't fail until you give up. Failure is not bad. It just *is*. It is part of the endless process. One business idea goes away, only to be replaced by another more exciting prospect. If you are to "be" who God wants you to be, then take life's little chastisements (take His, too) and get going again. There is power in motion.

If you take this to heart you can't fail. I realize many people think of great things, some have success in the back of their mind for years; some repeatedly set goals and then never do anything. They stop. Fear perhaps. Not wanting to fail—too many bad things can happen if they don't make it. It is all nonsense.

I have failed. Yes, it hurt. Yes, it gave some people the right to say, "I told you so," and though it was very unpleasant, I learned from it. I have made available in writing a lot of things that went wrong, how I could have changed or avoided them, and how I have avoided them in my current business.

(Note: I have a business symposium for would-be business owners and current business own-

*ers on how to grow a hundred million dollar busi-
ness—call 1-800-872-7411 for more information.)*

"To be thrown upon one's own re-
sources, is to be cast into the very lap
of fortune; for our faculties then un-
dergo a development and display an
energy of which they were previously
unsusceptible."
—Benjamin Franklin

The main thing I learned is that never again
would I set stupid goals. The whole goal setting
process made me leery—I would work on quality.
I would start with me, improve, change, but I would
start again. I would be successful by doing what
successful people do.

This leads up to my second reason for not liking the traditional way for setting goals. I like the
words "make goals" because this forces me to think
about making them. How do you make something?
You start with ingredients and figure out (by recipe,
or trial and error) how to put the ingredients together.

NO LIMITS
I am looking out at my ranch that is simply
beautiful. I have a high quality car. I have an
incredible business, with talented employees and
friends. We have huge investments in quality
things.

Everything I just mentioned is really more than I've ever hoped for. My dreams, my sights, my horizons are ever expanding. I don't want you to think that this just happened. I'm shocked by how fast it happened, but there is design to it all.

I love dreaming. I'm a big believer in day-dreams. I love talks with people about big, noble dreams. Many years ago, I said I would like to build a billion dollar company. Everyone, including my family, shot me down. "Why?" They asked. At first I tried to defend it. "Because, it's there (like Mt. Everest)." "Because I can do it," so few people can. "Because I've got what it takes—God has blessed me with talents and abilities, and if I keep Him first, my family second, and this business third, it will just happen." I would be remiss not to turn my talent over to "the exchangers or the banks" (Matthew 25 and Luke 19). I can develop this business and help tens of thousands of people.

Late one night on a lonely flight home, I penciled it out. We took our company public in May of 1993. Typically, over-the-counter stocks trade for 40 times earnings, some at 60 and 80 times. An average New York Stock Exchange company trades at just under 20 times earnings.

So you can understand what I set out to do, let me explain those multiples. All company stocks are valued at some multiple of what it is earning. Total all the stocks say, 10,000,000 in a company and multiply it by the current share price, say $20 and you would have a valuation of $200,000,000. This is called the market-cap, short for market capitalization.

"Whatever that be which thinks, understands, wills, and acts, it is something celestial and divine."

—Marcus Tullius Cicero

If this company has a $5,000,000 profit, it would be trading at 40 times earnings. If its earnings were $10,000,000 it would be at 20 times earnings (20 x $10,000,000 = $200,000,000) or have a P/E of 20. P/E means earnings per share.

Another way of looking at this is to take the $10,000,000 earnings and divide by the amount of shares outstanding, also 10,000,000. Each share is making $1. If the stock costs $20, the $1 represents a $1 profit, or 5%. Investors are willing to pay $20 to get $1 of earnings (whether these earnings are paid out or not). In the aggregate, investors are willing to pay $200,000,000 in stock to get at $10,000,000 or $5,000,000 or whatever. Sometimes the company makes no money; people are betting on a turnaround, or future profits.

How do you find this? Ask any stockbroker what the P/E is, or what the earnings per share

are. They say things like, "This company is trading at 12 times earnings," or at "68 times earnings." You go from there.

Now with that semi-brief explanation, come back aboard the plane with me. Our company was grossing about $2,000,000 back then (about 2½ years ago). At the time this book was written, we were just under $10,000,000 per month. We are laying the foundation, by expansion, new products, hotel and real estate investments, to do a lot more than this.

"That's why the passion, the enthusiasm in our company is so high—we help so many people achieve their dreams."

—Wade Cook

Here's what I calculated. If our stock were to trade at 20 times earnings (again many companies in a growth mode trade at 40 times and more), and there's no guarantee it ever will, we would need to net $50,000,000. $50 million times 20 would be $1,000,000,000.

There it was in black and white. If the stock traded at 10 times earnings we'd have to net $100,000,000. If it traded at 40 times earnings it would only have to be $25,000,000.

There's my goal. $50,000,000. Run a great company and the stock price will follow. No fanfare—just build a great company.

I checked where we were. All we would have to do is get our sales up to $15,000,000 to $18,000,000 a month, keep control of expenses and bring $50,000,000 to the bottom line.

The stock price would take care of itself. And you know it really doesn't matter if we grow to a $800,000,000 or a $1.5 billion company. It's the process that is fun.

The next day, I launched the process. We doubled on advertising, we looked for more people, we started to find new phone systems, computers, and we looked for a new building (we moved into it in January of 1997). We also started investing in hotels, mortgages, other businesses—in the name of diversification and cash flow.

I hardly ever think about the $1 billion company. I'm too busy making it happen.

About a year ago a major national figure asked me what my goals were. I have set no limits. $1 billion, $12 billion who knows. He wanted a definitive answer. I said, "I don't have any, I'm enjoying myself and I just want to keep going, to do more of what I'm already doing. If you want to call that a goal, then fine. I call it "be-ing" the kind of person who improves, dreams, ponders, then improves some more." The road goes both directions—up and down. I want to stand before God and have Him say, "Well done thou good and faithful servant." That's why the passion, the enthusiasm in our company is so high—we help so many people achieve their dreams. I don't need a silly, limiting goal to do this. I need to be that kind of person.

SUBSTITUTE FOR REAL ACTION

What I just wrote, how I got it going, is my answer to this problem of substitution. Talk is cheap. What if I said I was going to build a billion dollar company and then did nothing?

You know, for about 1½ years I didn't tell anybody. Anytime I started the conversation they would put me down. I told myself I would have to make them believers. When we hit $3½ to $4 million a month consistently I mentioned it to my management staff. I showed them the numbers where we were when I first wrote the numbers, where we were then. By this time everyone had seen so much growth, so many miracles that they were easy to convince. All we have to do is three

---

"Nothing succeeds so well as success."

—Alexander A. Talleyrand-Perigord

---

to four times more sales. It was achievable, and again, as of this writing, we're well on our way. Our stock price has doubled in the last year, and with God's help we will continue to "be" good in the lives of our students and customers.

We don't need a failure-inducing, limiting, and stifling goal setting process to bring us down. We just have to walk the walk.

"The great high-road of human welfare lies along the old highway of steadfast well-doing; and they who are the most persistent, and work in the truest spirit, will invariably be the most successful; success treads on the heels of very right effort."
—*Samuel Smiles*

A Psalm of Life

Tell me not, in mournful numbers,
Life is but an empty dream!
For the soul is dead that slumbers,
And things are not what they seem.

Life is real! Life is earnest!
And the grave is not its goal;
Dust thou art, to dust returnest,
Was not spoken of the soul.

Not enjoyment, and not sorrow,
Is our destined end or way;
But to act, that each to-morrow
Find us farther than to-day.

Art is long, and Time is fleeting,
And our hearts, though stout and brave,
Still, like muffled drums, are beating
Funeral marches to the grave.

In the world's broad field of battle,
In the bivouac of Life,
Be not like dumb, driven cattle;
Be a hero in the strife!

Trust no Future, howe'er pleasant;
Let the dead Past bury its dead!
Act, - act in the Living Present;
Heart within, and God o-erhead!

Lives of great men all remind us
We can make our lives sublime,
And, departing, leave behind us
Footprints on the sands of time;

Footprints, that perhaps another,
Sailing o'er life's solemn main,
A forlorn and shipwrecked brother,
Seeing, shall take heart again.

Let us, then, be up and doing,
With a heart for any fate;
Still achieving, still pursuing,
Learn to labor and to wait.

—Henry Wadsworth Longfellow

8:
Biblical Words and Priorities

"If God be for us, who can be against us?"

—Romans 8:31

The directness and simple power of words used in the Bible is very impressive. There are numerous commands given, but God's words contain a few basic characteristics that God wants us to have and to do. Look at this list.

Love: love God, love one another. Treat each other well. "If ye love me, keep my commandments." I John 14:15

Obey: keep the word. Walk uprightly. Learn God's law and love it (see Psalm 119).

Serve: by charity, by love. "Inasmuch as ye have done it unto one of the least of these my brethren, ye have done it unto me." Matthew 25:40

Endure: stick with it. It won't be easy, but the journey is worth it.

God's ultimate "goal" is to bring us back to Him. Look at all He has done: this earth, prophets, scriptures, prayer, guidance by the Spirit, and almost unfathomable redemption. There is no half hearted approach, no lip service. What can we learn from the writings and stories of these ancient men and women?

"Everybody finds out, sooner or later, that all success worth having is founded on Christian rules of conduct."

—Henry Martyn Field

Life was intense. There were clear cut rewards and curses. They knew where they stood. So do we.

They were called upon to choose. The Bible is full of choices. "Choose ye this day whom you will serve ... as for me and my house, we will serve the Lord." (Joshua 24:15) Powerful words: choose, serve. It doesn't say, "Call a committee and figure out the easy road, or what feels good, or what short cuts to take."

They overcame unbelievable odds. The deck was stacked against them, but when obedient, they overcame. Armies were stacked against them; sin was rampant; people possessed their land; hatred of God's people was strong—yet story after story…

They were stubborn. Even God's chosen people fell away. Pride, sin, laziness, envy, and strife entered the picture. Moses's story tells it all. It is his battle to bring the people out of sin (bondage in Egypt is a metaphor) to peace and happiness (righteousness) ("land of milk and honey" is real, but to me a reverse metaphor). Yes, they need to leave Egypt, but just as important, they had to turn to God. Their struggle and our struggle is the same: turn to God and be right with Him.

"When God is for us who can be against us?"

The struggle with family problems. Parents loving, caring for, and when kids fall away, praying for their return. Real life reads like so many novels. Read of Abraham's love for Isaac. Read about Isaac sporting with Rachel. Lazarus, Martha and Mary, Adam and Eve, and even Moses and Aaron. Read about the prodigal son.

Very seldom do you have to question where people stood. They were either for God or against Him. I think all of us are consistently moving in one direction or the other. We are moving closer to good things, or away from them. I don't think anyone is so evil, so decrepit that he or she can't turn around, repent and make changes for the good. Likewise, I don't see anyone so righteous that they can't stumble and fall.

In this case direction is very important. God wants us to choose. "I know thy works, that thou art neither cold nor hot: I would thou wert cold or hot.'" (Revelation 3:15)

There is power in words. We can use these words: love, obey, serve, and endure; add to them patience, humility, vigilance, kindness, and so many others to help us set our priorities, keep our feet planted on a sure path, and fight the fight.

I took a little time out to look up a few words. Again, the word "goal" is nowhere to be found. Look at the powerful meaning of these words used in these scriptures.

Matthew 5:48 - Be ye therefore perfect, even as your Father which is in heaven is perfect.

I've written on this elsewhere. Focus on "Be."

"No man can tell whether he is rich or poor by turning to his ledger.—It is the heart that makes a man rich.— He is rich according to what he is, not according to what he has."
—H.W. Beecher

Matthew 6:33 - . . . but seek ye first the kingdom of God, and his righteousness, and all these things shall be added unto you.

In marketing and good writing you're supposed to answer all the questions, "Who, what, where, when and why." Look at this exceptional verse. What = seek; who = you and me; when = first; what again = the Kingdom of God, and so there's no misunderstanding and to bring it to our level these words are added, "and his righteousness." Then consequences and rewards are spelled out: what = all these things, and what again = will be added unto you. Can anyone read this and misunderstand the meaning?

John 17:3 - And this is life eternal, that they might know thee, the only true God, and Jesus Christ, whom thou hast sent (again, a wonderful collection of specific words).

Philippians 3:14 - I press toward the mark for the prize of the high calling of God in Christ Jesus.

And then under the word "motivation" I found the following verses. Again, specific "do it" type instructions.

Proverbs 23:7 - "For as he thinketh in his heart, so is he: . . ." (this one is used so often I originally thought others made it up. It says a lot).

Matthew 6:1 - "Take heed that you do not your alms before men, to be seen of them ..."

Matthew 6:18 - "That thou appear not unto men to fast..."

Again, without being too redundant, this is one major point of this book. Don't do things for show. Don't trade words for real action.

Let's also explore Matthew 6:21. It says, "For where your treasure is, there will your heart be also." How true. Could the opposite also be eventually true; where your heart is your treasure (big or small, good or bad) will be—eventually. What is important to you? God wants all of us to choose.

"The man who succeeds above his fellows is the one who, early in life, clearly discerns his object, and towards that object habitually directs his powers. Even genius itself is but fine observation strengthened by fixity of purpose. Every man who observes vigilantly and resolves steadfastly grows unconsciously into genius."

—Edward George Bulwer-Lytton

In verse 24 of the same chapter he tells us we can't serve two masters. If we choose Him, and follow His ways then "all these things shall be added unto you (Matthew 6:33)."

"If"

If you can keep your head when all about you
Are losing theirs and blaming it on you;
If you can trust yourself when all men doubt you
But make allowance for their doubting too;
If you can wait and not be tired by waiting,
Or, being lied about, don't deal in lies,
Or, being hated, don't give way to hating,
And yet don't look too good, nor talk too wise;

If you can dream—and not make dreams your master;
If you can think—and not make thoughts your aim;
If you can meet with triumph and disaster
And treat those two imposters just the same;
If you can bear to hear the truth you've spoken
Twisted by knaves to make a trap for fools,
Or watch the things you gave your life to, broken
And stoop and build 'em up with wornout tools;

If you can make one heap of all your winnings
And risk it on one turn of pitch-and-toss,
And lose, and start again at your beginnings
And never breathe a word about your loss;
If you can force your heart and nerve and sinew
To serve your turn long after they are gone,
And so hold on when there is nothing in you
Except the Will which says to them: "Hold on!";

If you can talk with crowds and keep your virtue,
Or walk with kings—nor lose the common touch;
If neither foes nor loving friends can hurt you;
If all men count with you, but none too much;
If you can fill the unforgiving minute
With sixty seconds' worth of distance run—
Yours is the Earth and everything that's in it,
And—which is more—you'll be a Man, my son!

—Rudyard Kipling

9:
Hard-hitting Methods

"Set your priorities. Your first priority is to study what it takes to be successful."

—Wade Cook

I hope by now you have figured out that my whole approach to "life, liberty, and the pursuit of happiness" is different. Let me, in this chapter, pull out what I consider some of the best ideas and techniques for success.

I'll use money—success financially—as my theme. You can interject the word diet, success, "get to the Olympics" or whatever in its place.

Here are fifteen things you can do to get on and stay on the road to financial prosperity.

1) Choose carefully your words. The words you say to yourself will make or break you. The

words you say and hear from others will subtract from or add to your process. Say the words out loud. Write down your thoughts, write down methods and processes on how you'll get to where you want to "be."

> *"A man cannot speak but he judges and reveals himself.—With his will, or against his will, he draws his portrait to the eye of others by every word.— Every opinion reacts on him who utters it."*
>
> —Ralph Waldo Emerson

---

2) Memorize key maxims, words, poetry, thoughts. Memorizing is a wonderful method to help you get up the determination and to help you stick to the plan and resolve to endure. There is a host of great phrases to memorize found in the Bible. Start there. It is, after all, the best place.

3) Don't tell anyone. Make them believers by results, not by "hot air." If you want to be thin, start walking, and do what it takes.

Sometimes saying your dreams to unsupportive people can be detrimental. Hopefully, your spouse is supportive, but even there, actions speak louder than words. Don't let words become a substitute for action.

"We frequently fall into error and folly, not because the true principles of action are not known, but because for a time they are not remembered; he may, therefore, justly be numbered among the benefactors of mankind who contracts the great rules of life into short sentences that may early be impressed on the memory, and taught by frequent recollection to occur habitually to the mind."

—Samuel Johnson

---

4) Set your priorities. Your first priority is to study what it takes to be successful. Your second priority is to put God, your family and your career in the proper order, then it's a matter of wise use of your time.

5) Study and learn from others. Surround yourself with successful people. Join groups—get involved in a MLM (Multi-Level Marketing) company if you have to—find people who are upbeat, on the go.

6) Be careful though, that you filter advice. Too much bad advice is given by people who talk the talk. If you want to make one hundred thousand dollars a year, why are you talking to anyone about money who is making less than one hundred thousand dollars a year?

7)   Concentrate on quality. Be a quality person. Do quality things. Invest in quality companies. Build a quality life. Don't accept mediocrity. Spend quality time with good books, good people, and good advisors. Be a class act.

"Show me the man you honor, and I will know what kind of a man you are, for it shows me what your ideal of manhood is, and what kind of a man you long to be."

—Thomas Carlyle

---

8)   Be a perpetual student. Never quit learning. Study and then study some more. Feed your brain "good junk." Develop a passion for learning. Work on your resolve to keep it. Truly, leaders are readers. And if you know what you want this education to do for you, what you want it to accomplish, you'll be a step ahead.

9)   Decide your highest and best use. You can't do it all, so excel at what you do. Hire, train, work with others to accomplish the rest.

"Be aware—new opportunities are everywhere."

—Wade Cook

---

10) Involve your family. Build a family dynasty. It can be your well oiled machine.

11) Forgive someone. There are many principles of success which I covered in **Business Buy the Bible**. In this book on "be-ing," I can think of no greater method of finding happiness and be-

---

"Our principles are the springs of our actions; our actions, the springs of our happiness or misery. Too much care, therefore, cannot be taken in forming our principles."
—Philip Skelton

---

ing successful than the principle of forgiveness. I'm assuming, obviously, that all of us make mistakes and need to change our lives. If so, then we, ourselves, need forgiveness. Follow this reasoning: whatever we measure out, it shall be measured to us again. ". . . with what measure ye mete, it shall be measured to you again." (Matthew 7:2; Mark 4:24; Luke 6:38)

It is an incredible cleansing process. It will help keep us humbled and right with God. It might be painful, but is definitely worth it.

12) Be aware—new opportunities are everywhere. Possibilities abound and it is wise to think

through all foreseeable ramifications. Think of serendipity and how discoveries are made. Be a "possibility" thinker. Ask yourself, "What other uses might this have? What can this friendship mean? How do we use this to build that?"

Awareness is a wonderful characteristic to develop.

13) Be industrious. Industry is the action which brings achievement. Consider the Bible scripture of the ant, "Go to the ant, thou sluggard. Consider her ways and be wise." (Proverbs 6:6) Wise in preparation, wise in dedication and in doing what it takes to survive—industry.

You've heard of captions of industry of old.

14) Grow out of your problems.

15) Be good to God and others.

"Man owes not only his services, but himself to God."

—Thomas Secker

"Set about doing good to somebody. Put on your hat, and go and visit the sick and poor of your neighborhood; inquire into their circumstances, and minister to their wants. Seek out the desolate, and afflicted, and oppressed, and tell them of the consolations of religion. I have often tried this method, and have always found it the best medicine for a heavy heart.

—John Howard

10:
Walk the Walk

"Don't settle for goals the old way."

—Wade Cook

There is a wonderful scripture—concise, powerful, and far-reaching that I'd like to use at the beginning of this conclusion.

"Commit thy works unto the Lord, and thy thoughts shall be established." Proverbs 16:3

The word "thoughts" is interesting. Substitute way, road, plan, or objective. The first part does not say "try" for commit, or "talk" for works. This is a whole different way of life if you live this scripture. It's in the right order. It doesn't say "establish your thoughts, then commit." It says "commit, then your thoughts will be set (established)." Again, God's priorities, His ways are much higher than ours, and His ways give us pause for thought.

I've seen a consistent problem with so many would-be successful people. It always seems that they need something they don't have, something outside themselves. "If only I had this or that, I'd be successful." It could be money, a day planner, attendance at a motivational seminar, or some

---

"Wilt thou draw near the nature of the gods? Draw near them then in being merciful; sweet mercy is nobility's true badge."
—William Shakespeare

---

nebulous goals. These things come and go, but go they will, and you're left with what? If you are to make it, you must change. Obviously, what you've tried up till now is lacking. It's time to try a new way.

If you can change your attitude then you'll have a chance. Dr. Laura Schlessinger, the famous radio host, said, "It is attitude, infinitely more than circumstance, that determines the quality of life." Powerful, oh, so powerful.

The applications and implications of my "dump the old ways" will clear your head. Now try goal getting, or my priority making strategies. Ultimately you'll master the science and art of BE-ING. <u>Don't</u> <u>set</u>tle for goals the old way. Life has

> "A man's ledger does not tell what he is, or what he is worth.—Count what is in *man, not what is* on *him, if you* would know what he is worth—whether rich or poor."
> —Henry Ward Beecher

infinitely more possibilities than stifling, discouraging, and limiting goal setting practices allow.

In short, you will be successful when you really like (or live) what you are doing. Yes, we may be a product of our conditioning and environment.

> "...God's priorities, his ways are much higher than ours, and his ways give us pause for thought."
> —Wade Cook

If, however, we want to rise above all of these, we have to learn the "how to," the "what to" and then get on with it. If you don't like what you're doing you'll probably never be successful. All the goals in the world can't overcome a dislike for what you're doing, or what you must do to make it.

BE. That's the key. Just be and work at BE-ING better at it.

"He is of the earth, but his thoughts are with the stars. Mean and petty his wants and desires; yet they serve a soul exalted with grand, glorious aims,—with immortal longings,—with thoughts which sweep the heavens, and wander through eternity. A pigmy standing on the outward crest of this small planet, his far-reaching spirit stretches outward to the infinite, and there alone finds rest."

—Thomas Carlyle

P.S. It's now 8:15AM on Monday; the book is done.

This is the way to get goals!

Appendix A: Results, Action, and Living

I went on a search for the word "goal." I mentioned in the book that it was not to be found in the Bible. "Oh, but the concept is there," I was told. "Go find it," I answered. Look up the word "objective" and "motivations" and you'll find references to the scriptures I mentioned in chapter eight. Notice how powerful verbs are used: "seek," "knock," "go," "be," and the like. One would have a hard time making a credible case for the concept of goal setting as it is used by our current motivational speakers.

I went to current "Quotes" books and there are some references. However, on one of my serendipity days, I found a book, "Serendipity of the

Spirit" published in 1877. The quotes, maxims, thoughts, et cetera, were collected from American and other European writers, politicians, statesmen and philosophers in the early history of our country's birth and infancy. Some went back hundreds of years before Christ's birth.

There were hundreds of topics. Most of the standard topics were included: honesty, perseverance, wealth, zeal; but there were others which we don't even talk about today.

Guess what? The word "goal," either as a topic heading, or all by itself was not to be found. It was difficult to see a corresponding idea to the "New Year's Resolution," or other goal setting methods of today.

These wise giants of the past just seemed to live the life they talked of. They put emphasis on results, action and living and giving for the good life. These words and advice seem much closer to God's words than to the words found in the current "self-help" books.

Oh, and before I forget, there was another by-product of this search. I found many current thoughts and maxims in the words of yesteryear. Look at this one, "One sign of craziness is to do ordinary things and expect extraordinary results."

My goodness, I thought it was a statement made in the 80's at some network marketing meeting, not out of a book published in the nineteenth century.

As far as I can tell, the word "goal," and the modern concept of "goal setting" could not be found until American football became really popular and widespread (TV made it so), say, in the later forties and fifties. "Touchdown!" "He crossed the goal line!" "Make the goal." "First and goal to go." Now part of Americana. I think that in many regards this new talk is very helpful. Football, though dangerous as it is, is full of lessons:

- Teamwork, pulling together, working it out, doing your part.

- Fan involvement, both financially and emotionally.

- First and ten, small bite size pieces.

- Strategies, both offense and defense.

- Developing talents.

- Being more than you set out to be.

- On and off-field action which develops character.

- Players and coaches working together to achieve great things.

If typical "goal setting" works like a well oiled football team, then fine. If it's just talk with no practice, determination and implementation, then I'd rather just sit back and enjoy watching others play the game.

Appendix B: Notes From Our Students

I wanted to put the actual words of our students in this book to show you what they do, what changes they've made and the difference knowledge of methods has made in their lives.

"The fabulous fact of man's ability to act, the wonder of <u>doing</u>, is no less amazing than the marvel of being.

—Abraham Joshua Heschel

Anyone can see what I do; my life is an open book, but to see the changes made in the lives of our students—ah, that is where miracles are found.

I decided to put these testimonials outside the regular book format. So here they are in an appendix.

Look at what they say about what they have learned and are now able to do.

Prior to the seminar, using Wade's strategies that I learned in Zero to Zillions, I made a net profit of $40,000 in about 40 days.

—John P.

After spending years purchasing "name brand" stocks, I attended the Wall Street Workshop. The day of the Workshop we learned of a stock that had split and purchased 1,000 shares. 4 weeks later we sold this stock for a $4,000 profit. The next month we tried covered calls on stocks we have been holding for years. Result - $2,200 in our pocket and we weren't called out of even one share. To date, following WIN, we have made about $20,000 in 4 months. I know this isn't anywhere near your biggest success but it has made a tremendous difference in how we now view our future. Thanks a million $$$$$$.

—Dennis S.

Now look at the changes made in these people's lives.

I've dreamed of being able to write one of these letters. Where do I start but to say that I attended the March 9-11 Wall Street Workshop in Santa

Barbara. This is my second workshop. The first time I didn't follow through, but before attending this seminar I decided to just follow directions and "follow the formulas"—period.

I started my account with $2,000 the day before the seminar and made two trades before noon. I did not put in additional money until March 24, and now have a total of $12,450 invested. I've made a total of five covered call plays and two options plays, and have already made $5,100 (over 40%) and the month is not even out. I will make two additional plays before the month's expiration date. If I get called out on the stocks that I should, I will be over a 50% profit in one month. The amazing thing, is that this last week the stock market has gone down more than any other week in years and I still make money!

I'm excited and will share this with others. I'm already going to sponsor some others to the next local Wall Street Workshop. This is going to change my life. Thanks for sharing all the information you have learned. I only hope I can change other lives as your class has changed mine with the knowledge I now have.

—Brian G.

On April 9, 1997, I started trading on behalf of a Foreign Corporation with $37,000. As of April 22, 1997, 10 days later, I have received cash in account of $16,739.67 (this is net—minus commissions). That's a 45% return in 10 days. Annualizing it out, it becomes 1,620%. But that's not the good news.

What this has allowed me to do is spend more time working our charitable foundation. I work about one hour in the morning on the stock market, one hour at lunch and then one hour at night preparing for the next day. (The foundation was set up to make grants to organizations that facilitate Judeo-Christian values especially as relating towards families.)

I praise the Lord for the education that we received from Wade Cook's organization (especially Paul Cook) and I cannot believe that we have done 54 trades and have only lost on one so far.

Thank you for the knowledge.

—Douglas Y.

I started making money on the second day of the Wall Street Workshop. I have nearly recovered the price of the seminar, hotel expenses, and airline tickets from Germany. I'm on my way! Thank you.

—Lawrence K.

You said in your tapes that we may well be able to make back the cost of the workshop during the workshop. Well I just wanted to tell you that I have made well over twice the cost of the workshop during the last two weeks and I haven't been yet! (I am registered to attend in a couple weeks.) My wife has had just one reaction to all of this: "Give up your day job!"

—Jim V.

My name is Judith C. and I am one of the students who attended the Wall Street Workshop on June 12-14, 1997. To date I have made $11,000!!! with a $2,000 investment in the stock market. I have never made any money like that in a week with my job or with any of the small investments I have. I am so excited I am unable to sleep at night.

I was laid off from a job I held for five years a week before I attended the seminar. I was so sad I was getting ready to call my sales representative and tell her I needed a refund. . . . I am so happy I decided to go. Everything is so wonderful I do not want to work for anyone anymore.

Once again, thanks for everything.

—Judith C.

And if you need a whopping big chunk of money look at what these people wrote:

I bought the Wall Street Money Machine back in September 1996 and opened an option and margin account immediately after reading the book. My first forays into the market were with covered calls and I have done quite well. Recently, I subscribed to the WIN network and have made over $10,000 in the past month with news that I received from WIN alone. The most recent was with Dell Computer. I saw where you guys had bought calls on Dell based on rumors of an impending stock split. I decided to buy both June 100 and June 105 calls the day before the date of *the rumored split. I invested $7,000 in these options and sold them less than 24 hours later for a profit of $7,625, a 109% return in 24 hours (a 39,700% annual return). Thanks WIN!*

—Lelton W.

What are they talking about? It's our "experiential learning"—"do the deals"—workshop. You should attend. It is a wonderful event and you'll never BE the same, financially.

Here are a few of the topics covered at the Wall Street Workshop:

Getting Started:
Strategies of Engagement, 5-Step Process of Wealth, Trading Basics, Trading Criteria, Making Effective Decisions, Return/Yield Calculation.

Rolling Stock:
Rolling options.

Options:
Vocabulary, LEAPS®, Options/News, Gathering Information, and How to Avoid Losses in Options.

Stock Splits:
Basics and Straight Stock Plays.

Writing Covered Calls:
Definition, the Wade Cook Covered Call Formula, Three Rules of Covered Call Writing.

Selling Puts:
Tandem Plays, Stacking the Deck in Your Favor, and Knowing When To Sell.

Peaks and Slams:
Dead Cat Bounce.

Bottom Fishing:
News Issues, Turnarounds, Spin-offs, and Penny Stocks.

Tax Wise Investing:
Section 42, Section 29, Entity Structures, and Retiring Rich.

For information on these and our books, please call us at 1-800-872-7411.

Appendix C: Continue Your Education

I have challenged you to BE, to DO, and to SHOW by your actions how you are going to GET your goals. In this appendix, I'll show you how I have, from my own experience, implemented successful and practical ideas into books, videos, and audio cassettes for your continuing education in the stock market, entity integration, and real estate. New ideas and techniques come along and laws continually change, so we're always updating our catalogue.

To order a copy of our current catalogue, please write or call us at:

Wade Cook Seminars, Inc.
14675 Interurban Avenue South
Seattle, Washington 98168-4664
1–800–872–7411

I mentioned my web site in an earlier chapter. The internet address is **http://www.wadecook.com**, and Lighthouse Publishing Group, Inc., the publishing company who published this book has an address at **http://www.lighthousebooks.com**.

I would love to hear your comments on our products and services, as well as your testimonials on how these products have benefited you. I look forward to hearing from you!

Stock Market

Stock Market materials I've produced include: ***Income Formulas***. This is a free cassette where you will learn the 11 cash flow formulas taught in the Wall Street Workshop. Learn to double your money every 2½ to 4 months.

My book, ***Wall Street Money Machine***, appearing on the *New York Times* Business Best Sellers list for over one year, contains the best strategies for wealth enhancement and cash flow creation you'll find anywhere for generating cash flow through the stock market.

Read **Stock Market Miracles** next, and you'll find that it improves on the strategies from **Wall Street Money Machine**, as well as introducing new and valuable twists on our old favorites.

Bear Market Baloney is a timely book! My predictions came true while the book was at press! Look into what makes bull and bear markets and how to make exponential returns in any market.

The **Dynamic Dollars Video** is the 90 minute introduction to the basics of my wall street formulas and strategies. Designed especially for video, I explain the meter drop philosophy, Rolling Stock, basics of Proxy Investing, and Writing Covered Calls.

A powerful audio workshop, **Zero To Zillions** will help you in understanding the stock market game, playing it successfully, and retiring rich. Learn eleven powerful investment strategies to avoid pitfalls and losses, catch "day-trippers," "bottom fish," write covered calls, double your money in one week on options on stock split companies, and so much more. I will teach you how I make 300% per year so that you can do likewise.

The **Wall Street Workshop** video series will help you get a head start if you can't make it to the Wall Street Workshop. Ten albums containing eleven hours of intense instruction on Rolling Stock, Options on stock split companies, Writing Covered Calls, and eight other tested and proven strategies designed to help you earn *18% per month* on your investments. By learning, reviewing, and implementing the strategies taught here, you will gain the knowledge and the confidence to take control of your investments, and double their value every $2^1/_2$ to 4 months.

The Next Step video series is presented by my Team Wall Street instructors, and is the advanced version of the Wall Street Workshop. Full of my power-packed strategies, this is not a duplicate of the Wall Street Workshop, but a very important partner. The methods will supercharge the strategies taught in the Wall Street Workshop and you'll learn how to find the stocks to fit the formulas through technical analysis, fundamentals, home trading tools, and more.

Wealth Information Network (WIN) is our subscription internet service which provides you with the latest financial formulas and updated entity structuring strategies. New, timely information is entered several times a day. If you are just getting started in the stock market, this is a great way to follow people who are proven successes. If you are experienced already, it's the way to confirm your feelings and research with others who are generating wealth through the stock market.

Subscribing to *WIN+* will ensure that Team Wall Street will email you with timely updates and information that you can't afford to miss. This is a must for anyone who cannot spend all day searching the web for time-sensitive information.

Information Quest is a paging system which beeps you as events and announcements are made on Wall Street. The key to the stock market is timing. Especially when you're trading in options, you need up to the minute (or second) information. However, most investors cannot afford to sit at a computer all day looking for news. We recognized this need and came up with an incredible and innovative solution—**IQ Pager.** You'll receive information such as major stock split announcements, earnings surprises, or any other news that will impact the market.

This new product is selling like crazy. Just imagine sitting in a meeting during the day and having the pager go off! Within minutes and sometimes before it hits the news wire you could know about a stock split. 200 characters of information show up on the pager, so it gives you enough to get you at least involved in a timely manner. We don't make any claims that we get every stock split or every piece of good news announced out there, but we sure get a lot of them. Right now the pagers are going off between 5 to 15 times a day, so I believe it is very much appreciated. If you want to get on board, you need to call your representative at 1-800-872-7411 and talk to them about getting the **IQ Pager.**

Entity Integration

Have you ever considered entity integration? I recorded *Power Of Nevada Corporations*, a free audio cassette where you'll learn that Nevada Corporations have secrecy, privacy, minimal taxes, no reciprocity with the IRS, and protection for shareholders, officers, and directors. This is a powerful seminar.

I created *The Incorporation Handbook* so you could make incorporation easy! This handbook tells you who, why, and, most importantly, how to incorporate. Included are samples of the forms you will use when you incorporate, as well as a step-by-step guide from the experts.

The *Financial Fortress Home Study Course* is an eight-part series in entity structuring. It goes far beyond mere financial planning or estate planning, and helps you structure your business and your affairs so that you can avoid the majority of taxes, retire rich, escape lawsuits, bequeath your assets to your heirs without government interference, and, in short, bomb proof your entire estate. There are six audio cassette seminars on tape, an entity structuring video, and a full kit of documents.

Come to our *Business and Entity Skills Training (BEST),* presented by me and the Team Wall Street instructors. You will learn about the six powerful entities you can use to protect your wealth and your family. Learn the secrets of asset protection, eliminate your fear of litigation, and minimize your taxes.

Real Estate

Are you interested in operating your own real estate money machine? My free cassette, **Income Streams**, will instruct you how to buy and sell real estate the Wade Cook way. This informative cassette will instruct you in building and operating your own real estate money machine.

My first bestselling book, **Real Estate Money Machine**, reveals the secrets of my own system—the system I earned my first million from. This book teaches you how to make money regardless of the state of the economy. My innovative concepts for investing in real estate not only avoids high interest rates, but avoids banks altogether.

Do you want to become an expert money maker in real estate? I wrote **How To Pick Up Foreclosures** to show you how to buy real estate at 60¢ on the dollar or less. You'll learn to find the house before the auction and purchase it with no bank financing—the easy way to millions in real estate. The market for foreclosures is a tremendous place to learn and prosper! **How To Pick Up Foreclosures** takes my methods from **Real Estate Money Machine** and super charges them by applying the fantastic principles to already-discounted properties.

Owner Financing, is a short, but invaluable, pamphlet I wrote for you to give to sellers who hesitate to sell you their property using the owner financing method. Let this pamphlet convince both you and them. The special report, *"Why Sellers Should Take Monthly Payments,"* is included for free!

Real Estate For Real People is a priceless, comprehensive overview of real estate investing. This book teaches you how to buy the right property for the right price, at the right time. I explain all of the strategies you'll need, and give you twenty reasons why you should start investing in real estate today. Learn how to retire rich with real estate, and have fun doing it!

Do you want to personally achieved success after success in real estate like I did? **101 Ways to Buy Real Estate Without Cash** fills the gap left by other authors who have given all the ingredients but not the whole recipe for real estate investing. This is the book for the investor who wants innovative and practical methods for buying real estate with little or no money down.

Legal Forms is a set of pertinent forms I have collected, containing numerous legal forms used in real estate transactions. These forms were selected by experienced investors, but are not intended to replace the advice of an attorney. However, they will provide essential forms for you to follow in your personal investing.

Record Keeping System is my complete tracking system for organizing all of the information on each of your properties. This system keeps track of everything from insurance policies to equity growth. You will know at a glance exactly where you stand with your investment properties and you will sleep better at night.

Money Machine I & II is an audiocassette series with my system for creating and maintaining a real estate money machine. It will teach you the step-by-step cash flow formulas that made me and thousands like me millions of dollars. Call us and learn the benefits of buying, and more importantly, selling real estate.

Assorted Financial Wisdom

Now that I have offered my wall street, entity planning, and real estate strategies to you, I will also make available to you some assorted financial wisdom in the form of a free cassette. This one, ***Money Mysteries of the Millionaires***, will teach you how to make money and keep it. This fantastic seminar shows you how to use Nevada Corporations, Living Trusts, Pension Plans, Business Trusts, Charitable Remainder Trusts, and Family Limited Partnerships to protect your assets.

My ***Brilliant Deductions*** manual is coming out again, even better than before! Do you want to make the most of the money you earn? If you want to have solid tax havens and ways to reduce the taxes you pay, this manual is for you! I will teach you how to get rich in spite of the new tax laws. See new tax credits, year-end maneuvers, and methods for transferring and controlling your entities. Learn to structure yourself and your family for tax savings and liability protection.

Some of my top Wall Street Workshop instructors and I: David Elliott, Debbie Losse, Joel Black, Dan Wagner, Scott Lamm, and Dave Wagner, have joined together to create *Blueprints For Success* a compilation of chapters on building wealth through your business and making your business function successfully. The chapters cover education and information gathering, choosing the best business for you from all the different types of businesses, and a variety of other skills necessary for becoming successful. Your business can't afford to miss out on these powerful insights!

Your business cannot succeed without you. This course, *High Performance Business Strategies,* will help *you* become successful so your company can succeed. It is a combination of two previous courses, formerly entitled Turbo-Charge Your Business and High-Octane Business Strategies. For years, my staff and I have listened to people's questions, and concerns. Because we know that problems are best solved by people who already know the ropes, my staff wanted to help. They categorized the questions and came up with about 60 major areas of concern. I then went into the recording studio and dealt head on with these questions. What resulted is a comprehensive collection of knowledge to get you started quickly.

Wealth 101 (1997) is my incredible book that brings you 101 strategies for wealth creation and protection that you can't afford to miss. From front to back, it is packed full of tips and tricks to supercharge your financial health. If you need to generate more cash flow, this book shows you how through several avenues. If you are already wealthy, this is the book that will show you strategy upon strategy for decreasing your tax liability and increasing your peace of mind through liability protection.

Turn your car into a "university on wheels" and listen to my ***Unlimited Wealth*** audio set. This is the "University of Money-Making Ideas" home study course that helps you improve your money's personality. The heart and soul of this seminar is to make more money, pay fewer taxes, and keep more for your retirement and family. This cassette series contains the great ideas from ***Wealth 101*** on tape, so you can listen to them whenever you want.

Is your IRA idle? Take that IRA money now sitting idle and invest it in ways that generate bigger, better, and quicker returns. ***Retirement Prosperity*** is a four audiotape set that walks you through a system of using a self directed IRA to create phenomenal profits, virtually tax free! This is one of the most complete systems for IRA investing ever created.

My good friend, John Childers' *Travel Agent Information* package is the only sensible solution for the frequent traveler. This kit includes all of the information and training you need to be an outside travel agent for a stable company. There are no hassles, no requirements, no forms or restriction, just all the benefits of traveling for substantially less *every time*.

Cook University:

People enroll in **Cook University** for a variety of reasons. Usually they are a little discontented with where they are—their job is not working, their business is not producing the kind of income they want, or they definitely see that they need more income to prepare for a better retirement. That's where **Cook University** comes in. As you try to live the American Dream, in the life-style you want, we stand by ready to assist you in making the dream your reality.

The backbone of the one-year program is the Money Machine concept—as applied to your business, to stock investments, or to real estate. Although there are many, many other forms of investing in real estate, there are really only three that work: the Money Machine method, buying second mortgages, and lease options. Of these three, the Money Machine stands head and shoulders above the rest.

It is difficult to explain **Cook University** in only a few words. It is so unique, innovative and creative that it literally stands alone. But then, what would you expect from Wade Cook? Something common and ordinary? Never! My staff and I always go out of our way to provide you with useful, tried and true strategies that create real wealth.

We are embarking on an unprecedented voyage and want you to come along. If you choose to make this important decision in your life, you could also be invited to share your successes in a *series* of books called ***Blueprints For Success*** (more volumes to come). Yes, it takes commitment. Yes, it takes drive. Add to this the help you'll receive by our hand-trained experts and you will enhance your asset base and increase your bottom line.

We want to encourage a lot of people to get in the program right away. You could save thousands of dollars if you don't delay. Call right away! Class sizes are limited so that students get personal attention.

Perpetual monthly income is waiting. We'll teach you how to achieve it. We'll show you how to make it. We'll watch over you while you're making it happen. Thank you for your consideration. We hope to see you in the program right away.

Cook University is designed to be an integral part of your educational life. We encourage you to call and find out more about this life changing program. The number is 1–800–872–7411. Ask for an enrollment director and begin your millionaire-training today!

If you want to be wealthy, this is the place to be.

Classes Offered:

The workshops I currently have to offer you are held all over the United States, including Hawaii and Alaska. ***Wall Street Workshop*** is presented by me and my hand trained instructors, Team Wall Street. The ***Wall Street Workshop*** teaches you how to make incredible money in all markets—tried-and-true strategies that have made hundreds of people wealthy.

Our ***Next Step Workshop,*** also presented by me and Team Wall Street, is an Advanced Wall Street Workshop designed to help those ready to take their trading to the next level and treat it as a business. This seminar is open only to graduates of the Wall Street Workshop.

Our ***Executive Retreat*** (with the same instructors as above) is created especially for the individuals already owning or planning to establish Nevada Corporations. The Executive Retreat is a unique opportunity for corporate executives to participate in workshops geared toward streamlining operations and maximizing efficiency and impact.

When you're ready, I hope to see you at the **Wealth Academy**, also presented by me and my Team Wall Street. This three day workshop defines the art of asset protection and entity planning. During these three days we will discuss, in depth and detail, the six domestic entities which will protect you from lawsuits, taxes, or other financial losses, and help you retire rich!

Call one of our representatives at Wade Cook Seminars, Inc. today and sign up for these workshops. The toll free number is 1-800-872-7411. See you there!